Creating Trance and Hypnosis Scripts

First published by O Books, 2009
O Books is an imprint of John Hunt Publishing Ltd., The Bothy, Deershot Lodge, Park Lane, Ropley,
Hants, SO24 0BE, UK
office1@o-books.net
www.o-books.net

Distribution in:	South Africa
	Stephan Phillips (pty) Ltd
UK and Europe	Email: orders@stephanphillips.com
Orca Book Services	Tel: 27 21 4489839 Telefax: 27 21 4479879
orders@orcabookservices.co.uk	
Tel: 01202 665432 Fax: 01202 666219	Text copyright Gemma Bailey 2008
Int. code (44)	
	Design: Stuart Davies
USA and Canada	
NBN	ISBN: 978 1 84694 197 9
custserv@nbnbooks.com	
Tel: 1 800 462 6420 Fax: 1 800 338 4550	All rights reserved. Except for brief quotations
	in critical articles or reviews, no part of this
	book may be reproduced in any manner without
Australia and New Zealand	prior written permission from the publishers.
Brumby Books	
sales@brumbybooks.com.au	
Tel: 61 3 9761 5535 Fax: 61 3 9761 7095	The rights of Gemma Bailey as author have
	been asserted in accordance with the
Far East (offices in Singapore, Thailand,	Copyright, Designs and Patents Act 1988.
Hong Kong, Taiwan)	
Pansing Distribution Pte Ltd	
kemal@pansing.com	A CIP catalogue record for this book is available
Tel: 65 6319 9939 Fax: 65 6462 5761	from the British Library.

Printed in the UK by CPI Antony Rowe

O Books operates a distinctive and ethical publishing philosophy in
all areas of its business, from its global network of authors to
production and worldwide distribution.
This book is produced on FSC certified stock, within ISO14001
standards. The printer plants sufficient trees each year through
the Woodland Trust to absorb the level of emitted carbon in
its production.

Creating Trance and Hypnosis Scripts

Gemma Bailey

BOOKS

Winchester, UK
Washington, USA

CONTENTS

Foreword by the Author

I first came into contact with the powers of hypnotherapy at a time when, like many others, I recognised the need for a Turning Point in my life. Having worked myself into a state of ill health I realised that whilst the bank manager was more than satisfied with my choice of career as a manager for a large company, I was not. It wasn't a small adjustment to my career path that I needed; it was a complete change of direction!

Several years on and I am happier and healthier than I have ever been. As a trainer of both Hypnotherapy and NLP for my training company People Building, it gives me great joy to share with others the skills I have acquired. This means that I am assisting other people in making the changes they wish to experience too, in both my therapy practice and my teaching. Some of these changes may be quite specific, such as becoming more confident when presenting to groups of people. Other changes may be global, such as learning a new skill that can help you use your mind and thoughts more effectively for better results in your life as a whole.

The benefits of hypnotherapy far outweigh the misconceptions about the subject. It is both safe and effective, and more than that, it is a natural state that anyone who is happy to relax, can utilise. This makes it a fascinating and yet simple skill to learn such that my enthusiasm for the subject has led me to collate all of the hypnosis scripts I have written for the many clients I have had the pleasure of treating.

I'm incredibly grateful to Karen Hastings, Adeline Munoz, Diane Bayfield and my Mum for their assistance in typing up and contributing to endless pages of these scripts. (This would all still be in the planning stages without their help!)

I must also extend my love and thanks to the supportive and encouraging members of my family, to KG, and The Itchy

1

Hedgehogs (you know who you are) whose belief in my dreams and aspirations has never wavered.

Even when I have driven them crazy.

Gemma Bailey.
D.Hyp M.NLP Certified Trainer of NLP & Hypnotherapy.

Founder of People Building, Co-founder of NLP4Kids.
Better Understanding of Yourself Now. Only With People Building.

Introduction

People are going into trance all the time. In many ways, it is a perfectly natural state that we all experience at different times. Some people go into a trance when they are driving - sometimes to the degree that when they get home, there are parts of their journey that they cannot remember experiencing. Some people go into a trance when watching a movie at the cinema and are able to delete the other people around them such as the noise that those people may be making whilst eating their popcorn. The light trance they experience means they are able to focus only on the movie. Hypnosis is a very focused state to be in and normally, the focus is on the sound of the hypnotherapist's voice and words. This can be extremely beneficial as suggestions for positive change can be made and are more readily accepted. During a hypnotic trance, a person's conscious mind (the logical, analytical part of your mind that is usually chattering away in the background) is "out of the way." What this means is that the state of deep relaxation that is coupled with hypnosis, causes the conscious mind to rest so that the suggestions are less likely to be rejected or disputed by the conscious mind.

A formal trance can be induced and deepened by using the scripts in this book found in the induction and deepener sections. An induction is particularly useful for helping the patient to begin relaxing their body. When the body is relaxed it is much easier for the mind to relax too. A deepener can then be used to make the trance even deeper than it was before. The deeper the trance is, the more likely it is that the suggestions will be accepted because the unconscious (where all automatic behaviours and habits are stored) can be accessed without the filtering of the critical conscious mind.

Once you have induced the trance you may like to think about offering some positive suggestions for change. This book contains tried and tested hypnosis scripts that have been written by a qualified hypnotherapist. The sentences have been designed using specific language patterns that are more likely to be accepted by the unconscious and to aid the trance experience. Some of the language patterns may read as if they are questions or statements, yet by changing the tone of your voice, you can make them sound like commands that you want the client to follow. These are called embedded commands and these are underlined in the scripts to help you to remember where to make your voice deeper and very slightly louder. Where possible, the suggestions are always stated in a positive way, to get the patient to focus on what it is you want them to do, instead of what you don't want them to do. This is because primarily, the unconscious does not process negatives within a sentence. So if I said to you "Don't think of the queen. Don't make a picture of her face on a blue stamp, or hear the sound of her voice or feel any feelings you might feel about the queen" then your mind has to first scan through all of your resources to find the information you have stored in your mind about the queen. When it finds it and focuses on it, it can then let it go. So not doing something is always going to be a two-step process, that involves firstly calling to mind the thing you are not supposed to be doing!

The scripts in this book have been labelled as either:

Amateur Use - These scripts can be used by anyone who is comfortable in inducing and deepening a trance experience. As with any therapeutic work, you should use these scripts only in a safe environment and in an ecological way. If you have any concerns about using these scripts with a client, or concerns about the client you are working with, you should refer them to a qualified professional.

or

Professional Use - These scripts are recommended for professional use only, due to the nature of the problem or the likelihood of abreaction (a physical or emotional reaction to the suggestions you have given.) There are times in a hypnotic session, when the professional hypnotherapist needs to adjust the script to accommodate the reactions of the client, and the scripts labelled as Professional use are more likely to evoke responses that require flexibility from the therapist.

Once you have induced and deepened your trance, used one or a combination of the scripts in this book, you will then need to end the trance session. To ensure you have brought your client back to their usual waking state, you could use something like the following:

"In a few moments it will be time to return to your normal waking state, feeling refreshed and energised. And as this happens, the suggestions I have given you will remain in the subconscious part of your mind, and will continue to cause positive changes for your betterment and wellbeing every day in every way. So as I count back from 5 up to 1, you will begin to feel more and more awake and alert, until, when I reach one, you will be fully and completely wide awake with your eyes open. Ready now, as 5,4,3,2,1 with your eyes open now and wide, wide awake."

Once you have become comfortable with using the scripts in this book, you might like to start creating your own hypnosis scripts to accommodate the needs of your patients. You will of course develop your own style of writing and delivery and can now do so knowing that you are utilising the hypnotic language patterns, and intonation sequences of a professional hypnotherapist. The last section of this book is designed to assist you in creating high quality hypnosis scripts using double binds, loops, metaphors and many other linguistic tools that are normally only available to learn via a professional diploma.

~

Hypnotic Inductions

~

Body Relaxation Induction

Amateur- This is a simple induction that works on the principle that when the body has relaxed, the mind can relax also.

Rest comfortably; draw attention to your breathing. Your breathing becomes slow, deep, rhythmic. Easing into deep a relaxed state. A bit like the one you experience just before falling asleep. Hearing and feeling, choosing to relax, able to drop down into complete relaxation at any given moment.

Resting comfortably there, eyes closed, safe and secure. Taking in deep breaths, deeply in, exhale slowly. And again and another.

Concentrate only on my voice now, put aside any other thoughts. I want you to draw attention to various parts of your body, I want you to relax every muscle, nerve and cell in that part of your body until it is totally, completely, pleasantly heavy. First of all let me draw your attention to your fingers, hands, wrists. Consider those areas and be aware of any tension.

Now relax those muscles, lengthen and loosen, relax them comfortably, very, very relaxed. When they are relaxed now, concentrate on your feet, ankles, calves and up to your thighs. Tensing if necessary and then relaxing, flowing, drifting away, every fibre in the legs and feet melting into complete, deep relaxation.

Aware now of your trunk, the stomach and chest becoming more and more relaxed. Drain away tension like sand pouring through an hourglass, through the shoulder, neck and scalp. Loose limp… relaxed… lengthening… heavy. Completely relaxed, continuing deeper… heavier… sinking… floating down. Drifting further with every word I say. Relaxing twice as much each time you hear me say "Deeper and deeper".

I want you to remember a special place, somewhere where you felt totally relaxed and at ease…

I'm going to count from 10 down to 1 and you will find that you relax even more deeply with each number that I count.

Complete relaxation peace of mind and body. Open and free to new suggestions. Complete comfort 10, <u>deeper and deeper</u>, 9 <u>drifting down deeper and deeper</u>. <u>Feel settled, safe, secure</u>, relaxation working through you, 8 guided gently <u>down deeper and deeper</u>, 7 slow and easy each breath relaxing more, 6 <u>deeper and deeper</u>, 5 heavy and tired, body relaxed tired and heavy, 4 with each word <u>deeper and deeper</u>, 3 without concerns, nothing to bother you, concentrate on my voice, 2 the deepest point of relaxation ever, double that feeling down to 1, <u>resting peacefully</u>. Put aside any thoughts and problems. No demands. A time of silence.

Complete Relaxation
Amateur- This script offers the patient permission to allow themselves to relax. There are lots of opportunities to embed the command of relaxation throughout this script.

Now as you continue to rest back there, very comfortably, I'd like you to know how much I admire the way you have continued to keep going through all of the troubles and stresses that life has dealt you over the past time.

I'm sure there have been many times when you wish you could <u>just relax</u> and switch off from the outside world, or perhaps you have even been too preoccupied to even wish, just soldiering on, keeping going and having little time to give anytime for yourself. Well I want you to know that all of that is about to change, because you have made the wise and conscious decision to give time to yourself, to <u>repair yourself</u>, to <u>heal yourself</u> and <u>relax yourself</u>. That time is now and you can simply become <u>more comfortable</u> in this experience, safe in the knowledge that all that I say now, is for you, specifically and entirely for your own good and wellbeing.

So there are two of us now, fussing over you, <u>relaxing you</u>, there is me, here, gently guiding you into a restful place and you, there, drifting and just noticing those sensations of melting easily down. You may start to notice as you <u>breathe in</u>, the light, floating feeling that fills your body or perhaps the sense of gentle release as you <u>breathe out</u>. And as you notice these wonderful feelings I'd like you to think about how relaxed each and every parts of your body has become.

You can think of this totally and completely easily and let any other thoughts or words or pictures slip away as your mind drifts and fades. So begin now with your head. And the relaxation can flow into your forehead like a gentle wave down and across the face into your eyes, cheeks and your mouth until the mouth seems to <u>let go</u> of the jaw. <u>Let go</u> of all of the tension allowing the muscles and tissues to sag down, droop and relax. Let the relax-ation spread like a glowing warmth, perhaps you can see the colour of this relaxation as it dissolves past your ears and down the back of your head and as it meets your neck, the neck can <u>let go</u> and the head can just drift away on a short holiday.

Perhaps a beach or a tropical lagoon or an English garden filed with wild lavender. As the relaxation sinks deep into your neck I wonder what it would be like for all of the fibres and muscles in your neck and throat to deeply softly <u>comfortably relax</u>, let it <u>sink down</u> and into your neck, and as it reaches the shoulders, the shoulders <u>let go</u> and the necks drifts away on a short holiday.

Now the shoulders. Allow all of the tension to loosen and flow away between your shoulder blades and into your chest which releases any remaining tension with each outward breath. Down and down your back, deeper and deeper inside down your trunk and into your stomach and abdomen and then the pelvis, and as it sinks deeper inside of you, if your bones creak or crack or your stomach gurgles or groans then that is fine, each part can tell you it is relaxing.

And as this happens you will notice the simultaneous relax-ation as it drifts through your body, parallel with your arms. Letting that comfort <u>flow down</u> your arms, through and unknotting your elbows down to your wrists through your hands and each segment of each finger, right to the tips. As you notice now the heaviness of your legs, <u>they just sink down</u>, limply, comfortable. Imagining what it might look like to relax all of the tissue and all of the muscles in your thighs down to your knees <u>down, down</u> to your calves deeply and restfully moving through the ankles and finally your feet, imagine now removing a tight and uncomfortable pair of shoes from your feet and immersing your feet into cool healing water and your feet can soak in the healing water allowing its healing power to be absorbed and to travel to every part of your body.

~

Deepeners

~

Radio Metaphor

Amateur- This is a simple script that appeals to the unconscious of those who particularly enjoy listening to the radio, as it will offer a sense of familiarity. Counting is often used for deepening a hypnotic trance, and this script offers a new alternative in the use of numbers and levels.

For a while now you've been trying to take control of your life, to tune into a different frequency. It's time to start listening to the positive messages you hear, *now,* in the music of your life. Re-tune now, out of the confusion of the white noise to a different level of radio waves. You cannot see them, but you know they are there.

From this one life, tune up now from 98.8 to 99, 100, 101, 102, into smooth at 102.2 and <u>you'll be happier there</u>, that goal achieved, but soon you'll find that you want to grow louder and louder, turning up the volume on your life. And perhaps this new level of motivation will encourage you to explore <u>up and up</u>, beyond where you thought possible to 105.4. Where you will find magic.

And for a while magic is fulfilling, it gives you everything you wanted to see and feel and hear.

But <u>you're unconscious </u>- mind knows that in order to live, you must grow, and you're tuned in now to finding other air<u>ways</u>, so you progress to 106, and then 106.2 where you find heart.

Relaxing Inner-Self for Healing

Professional- This script encourages the deepening of the trance as the client's hand drifts down towards their lap. This script contains a *HAND LIFT* You will need to ask the client for permission to do this deepener before putting them into a trance so that you do not startle them by touching their hand whilst they are relaxed.

Now that you are <u>so deeply relaxed</u>, you can make wonderful and positive changes within your mind, <u>so easily and so simply</u>. You can begin to enjoy looking forward to a future free of pain and discomfort. Comfortable with yourself in a way that you can enjoy a feeling of being comfortable, a settled relaxation and calm of every inner muscle, organ, fibre and nerve within you.

Comfortable in your mind that you have tended to every thought sufficiently now. That it is time to let go of anxieties or worries from the past and time now to move forward into a positive and happy future that you will create for yourself. You will do this easily for yourself for that is what you want for yourself - to move forward - to look to the future as a place of renewed hope and comfort. Practice enjoying that internal relaxation, let it glow from the inside outwards as you call upon your complex inner mind to activate your vivid imagination, and see, hear and feel yourself in a scene of your future, in a place that is comfortable for you to be. Where you can see, hear and feel yourself as that calm and comfortable person in good health, confident and untroubled, enjoying your life, smiling, happy and well.

What will you hear, see and feel that tells you that you are calm and comfortable within your body? How will you look, stand, sound? What will you have that demonstrates your good health? How uplifted will you look as that comfortable person healed with a wealth of wellness? What will you do differently as that person? How will your life change - How many things can you create for yourself to look forward to? How good will you look and feel? You can create and improve this feeling of internal relaxation and practice it regularly, for what your mind can conceive, your mind can achieve.

In a moment I will lift your hand and as it drifts gently towards your lap changes will occur within your neurology and physiology. These changes will all be for your wellbeing and betterment. *LIFT HAND*

As you drift down deeper and deeper accept now that you are in control of your own thoughts and feelings and you accept the responsibility to ensure that these are always of the highest most positive, calming quality for yourself.

Relax and go down and down, feeling lighter as you desensitise any panic or anxiety or phobia or ill health, relaxing the tension that feeds these issues, allowing you to become lighter. And when your hand touches your lap, this is a signal to your subconscious mind to commence the appropriate changes - to put you in immediate control of your thoughts and feelings as you accept the responsibility to ensure that you do the very best for yourself, provide only the highest quality of thoughts and feelings in a calm positive quality and that in this new strength, this new control you banish all panic, tension, anxiety, phobia, ill health, cutting off the energy supply to the debilitating thoughts and emotions with a permanent defiance that is your own will, determination, strength and influence for good.

~

Weight Loss

~

Eat Less

Amateur - This script encourages the client to reduce their meal sizes and food intake to assist them with their weight loss. It can be used in conjunction with other weight loss scripts, or on its own.

Now as you <u>rest and relax</u>, just enjoy that wonderful lightness of mind and body. As you <u>breathe in</u>…. lighter and lighter.

Now you have told me before how much you enjoy your food and that is a good thing, yet it can become unhealthy to enjoy food when you do not know when to stop eating.

Everybody is born with a natural in-built ability to <u>know when their stomachs are full</u>. And you really do not need to eat nearly as much as you thought you needed to, in order to be full up.

The challenge is, things happen throughout life, circumstances, lifestyles mean that over time, we start to ignore our bodies' own signals, the messages to stop eating now. The warning signs over-ridden and we force in just an extra couple of mouthfuls, and the stomach expands, to accommodate the extra mouthfuls and then next time, was able to eat more, and another extra couple of mouthfuls - and so on.

<u>The time has come for that to change</u> - to reset that "stop eating now" signal to a healthy and appropriate level, where you can eat less and feel full. You wouldn't want to overfill yourself, as that leads to heavy, uncomfortable feelings, and you want to enjoy a lighter, freer and healthier feeling in your body now. You're unconscious mind has a blue print of your body in perfect health, fit, well, strong and at the correct weight, lighter than it is at present.

Go inside now and ask within your own mind for permission from your subconscious to alert you at the <u>appropriate time</u> to stop eating your meal when your body has received enough food to survive and flourish. And as you do this, note inside the positive feelings or sensations or messages that your subconscious mind creates as a positive response to your request. Now you have some responsibility here. That signal to stop eating that you have ignored for so long will be faint at first, perhaps unrecognisable above the clamour and clatter of other thoughts that have taken greater priority for so long now.

It is your responsibility to listen to your mind and body for that signal to "stop eating now" to occur. And when you hear it, respect it being there by following its instruction to stop eating now, and thank it for its assistance.

And if any part of you is urging you to override this signal you will be reminded in a manner that is instant and powerful as your subconscious mind helps you, and reminds you of your commitment to yourself, your total responsibility for your own health, your life, your own happiness. Allowing you to enjoy that lightness, a lighter mind, no longer burdened by thoughts of ill health, a lighter body that excess weight finally being burnt away.

And now maintaining your body in good health by listening to your body's own cues for hunger, when to eat and when to stop - the right food, the right amount at the right time. It's ok to leave food on your plate – waste goes in your bin, not on your waist.

Imagine in your mind, how your stomach looks inside your body - perhaps pinkish or orangey in colour, with soft flexible tubing neatly fitting inside your tummy. Now with this picture, I'd like you to see that with each number I count, the stomach shrinks smaller and lighter, less and less 5,4,3,2,1.

Chocolate Addiction
Professional - By focusing on chocolate in ways that are not normally experienced, the hypnotherapist can begin to draw the client's attention to the negative elements of consuming chocolate. This script therefore is likely to create an abreaction.

You have told me that you want to be free of this addiction which, not only interrupts your ability to control your own thoughts and actions, but is also beginning to have an impact on your health.

And it's not surprising is it?

Chocolate is made of fat. About 70% of the cocoa bean is fat alone. You know how chocolate becomes soft and tacky when warm, eventually becoming liquid, well what does that remind you of? Lard. A great solid chunk of lard from the fridge. Would you slice that up and eat it? Would you <u>feel it melting between your teeth</u> to then swallow down that slimy fat so that it can attach itself to the inside of your body. To your vital organs, slowing them down, until parts of you stop working for good. And then what will you say? "It's not my fault, I couldn't help it; it was out of my control…"

Now is the time for you to <u>take control and responsibility</u> for what you do and don't put into your body. You only have <u>this one body</u> and if you damage it for good, you will not be able to pop to the shops and get a new one.

So we're now going to change the way you think about chocolate. I want you to fully engage in this experience and allow your creative unconscious to guide you in the experiences that you will have now. Listen to my voice, the more you concentrate, the more powerful this experience will be. As such, this session will have such a profound and powerful impact upon the way you think about chocolate, in the future <u>you will find chocolate so completely disgusting, you will no longer want to eat it again</u>. There is only one way to deal with addictions, and that is to eradicate them completely. No cutting back, no sneaky little bits here and there, but instead, this problem gone for good, and you healthier, fitter and freer.

I want you to think about the way you think about chocolate. It's all about the memory of what this means to you and really has very little to do with the stuff itself. So we're going to change the way you keep that memory in your mind.

How do you remember chocolate? Perhaps you think about unwrapping it, and noticing if it's warm or very cold. If you like it warm, I'd like you to make it cold *solid* if it's cold solid, make it warm and tacky. That's it, the first little change. That was easy wasn't it? And at once you begin to notice. It's just not as good as it used to be.

Now relax, rest back and put a little in your mouth. Just let it melt down, or perhaps you like to chew and chomp at it quickly. If you like to chew it, let it melt instead, if you like to let it melt, I want you to chew it and just begin to change that experience again.

Now, I don't know if you've noticed this before, but you'll definitely notice it now....how the sugar creates that furry feeling on your teeth. Like a layer of scum, covering your teeth, gradually eating away at them, rotting them. You want to scrape it off, but you can't, not yet. It makes you think about how your teeth have ached in the past. That dull pain deep down in the nerves of your teeth from the sugar from the chocolate, slowing rotting them away in a layer of sugary scum.

Now take another bite. And notice, in your mouth, amongst the sticky brown ghew, mixed up with your saliva, a hair, clearly embedded in the chocolate, now in your mouth. And the hair is partially stuck in between your back teeth, so you cannot put your fingers in and get to it. In your efforts to do so, you swallow half the hair and it's now half way down your throat and half in your mouth. (Hypnotherapist- speed up as you speak, sound more intense) Causing you to gag and choke, the whole time with that tickling feeling of someone's hair from somewhere on their body caught in your throat and that taste of sweet sickly chocolate.

You choke so much that you gag and up comes a mouthful of chocolate that you swallowed earlier and you taste that chocolate- it's never as nice second time round. It has that acidic vomit taste about it, lumps in it and chocolate all mixed together. And there it is in your mouth, with the stray hair - but where will you go to spit it out?

Now you and I both know, that this can happen, in exactly the way I am telling you it will happen.

I will not tell you that you <u>will never eat chocolate again</u> or that the very thought of chocolate will <u>remind you of that taste of vomit, the hair in your mouth and that gagging feeling</u>. I would not tell you that. I will simply remind you of this: Your unconscious will do whatever it takes to protect and preserve your body, and should you ever put a chocolate product to your lips again, you will be instantly reminded in a most recognisable way, of your commitment to your health and body and you will surely think twice about eating chocolate again, that addiction, now gone.

Leverage for Motivation for Exercise

Amateur - Some people say that human beings are more motivated by pain than pleasure, so by getting the client to imagine their future in the way it would be if they continued to gain weight, will give them the motivation to start exercising. This should of course be used in addition to thinking about the positive implications of exercising so that there is also a positive goal to move towards.

As you rest and relax there I want you to start to reflect on the problem you have come here with today, and all of the excuses you have created to enable you to keep your problem. It's funny, that when people have this kind of a problem, they find it more painful to change, than the pain they have from doing the problem, so what we are going to do this is to apply more pain to your problem, to make your problem so unbearable that you <u>must stop</u> doing it.

You have told me that you really should be making more of an effort to get fit and go to the gym, that part of you wants to, but a bigger part of you really can't be bothered to, *that* part of you keeps making excuses. Now what I would like you to do is to just imagine a day in 12 months time, driving and as you pass the gym on your way, your eyes deliberately stick to the road ahead as if trying to delete the gym from your view, but you just notice that you're clutching the steering wheel a little tighter, and your heart beat has become stronger and slightly faster, as if there's a tension inside, and then you realise it's because in your mind, part of you is saying "maybe go to the gym today?" and the voice is so faint and so weak that you hardly even hear it, and you never even bother to pack your gym bag any more.

As you slow in the traffic you look down and notice that your clothes are feeling quite uncomfortable, they've felt like this for a while now, they're becoming increasingly tight. Your clothes are not shrinking, you are expanding. Your clothes are restricting you, uncomfortable and tighter and tighter.

Eventually you get home. You always feel so tired and sluggish these days, perhaps you need to relax, put the dinner on; and have a bath whilst it's cooking. So you go into the kitchen, and you're feeling hungry, so you search the fridge and the cupboards for something to munch on whilst you decide what to have for dinner. The shopping was done yesterday and there is so much to choose from - you seem to go through food much more quickly these days, perhaps it's because you're home every evening sitting around instead of exercising. Anyway you find a snack and put the dinner on, it's just you in the house and you prepare your bath whilst the oven is preheating.

Now notice, as you undo your clothes, the way your body seems to burst out of them, the releasing feeling as you undress. As you check your skin, you see indents on your body, the lines of the seams from your clothes have marked your skin, initially you think "my clothes are becoming too small" then another thought, "no, my body is getting bigger."

Now walk to a mirror and look at your body, how much weight have you added on in the last 12 months? Is it half a stone? Or a whole stone; or more? Notice how parts of your flesh seem to hang and sag and how other parts are becoming dimpled, lumpy and uneven. There even seems to be extra weight around your face and cheeks. For a moment you are struck with a sickening panic, the work that would have been so simple to correct 12 months ago, now seems less easy to achieve, as if <u>you've gone too far</u>. Disappointment grows inside you now, as you remember driving past the gym earlier. "They'd be no point in going anyway" - you tell yourself. "It's going to take a lot to burn all this off and it's easier to just cover it up." So you abandon your bath, as you cannot stand to look at your large limbs and tummy anymore - and desperately search your wardrobe for something comfortable, that you can still fit into, to wear but there are no really nice clothes in your size.

You wander around the house tidying up and preparing your dinner. As you wander around the house, cooking and tidying up, you keep wanting to just sit down. You know that stuff needs doing but you feel so tired these days, quite down and often wheezy. The fact that you're overweight and unhealthy obviously doesn't help but you don't like to think about that too much.

Now dissociate yourself from this scene and see yourself a further 12 months into the future. You're out shopping, it's been a tough week at work, you don't seem to be able to motivate yourself to get your work done and it's getting you in trouble. You could have gone shopping with your friends today, but they're out looking for new swimwear for a summer holiday and you can't wear swimwear anymore, you need to stay covered up on holiday these days, you're too gross to show your body. So you're going to treat yourself to a new wardrobe, will you need one, hardly anything fits you that you own and you're going to have to give it all to charity shops.

So you go into a shop, and find a few items in what you believe are your size. Take them to the changing room and try them on. First of all you must struggle to get out of your tight old clothes and then as you attempt to slip something on, you realise that it won't even fit around the tops of your wobbly round limbs, but you check the label, this is your size, it should fit, so you pull really hard but the material is too tight and is cutting into your skin and cutting off your circulation. So you start to try to take it off. You know you've put on weight, but their sizing must be wrong on the labels too! You are having great difficulty removing the clothing, you're fighting to get it off but are also concerned about damaging the item, in your panic you begin to grow hotter and hotter, sweatier and sweatier, you heart pounding and racing, your breathing and wheezing increasing. From outside, one of the sales staff hears your distress, and is coming into the changing room to ask what's wrong, to ask if you need help. You know you're not going to get out of this by yourself. You're going to have to ask for help, to help to undress you, because you didn't realise how fat you'd got and now you're stuck. You let the sales assistant into the changing room, reddening and babbling an apology. They sales assistant looks shocked and embarrassed, but pulls at the item and eventually manages to free you. Then asks if you'd like to try it on in a couple of sizes bigger, but in your distraught embarrassment you say no, get yourself together, and leave, close to tears. But I don't want you to think about that too much, because you might have lost your figure, and feel like the old you is is slipping through your fingers, but mostly you're sad because you've already lost yourself. That strong sense of who you are and what you're all about, now just a memory. Only disappointment for yourself and from others, remains.

Now step away from that image and just listen to the sound of my voice. My voice will drift with you wherever you go and wherever you go my voice will remain in the subconscious part of your mind.

You see the difference between failures and successful people, is that successful people do not believe their own excuses. <u>They do not believe their own excuses</u>. Have you ever felt so committed to something, perhaps a new relationship, which despite everyone else telling you it wouldn't work, you went ahead and did it anyway . . ? Or perhaps you really set your mind on achieving something so much so that you visualised yourself doing it really well and really easily, like imagining yourself doing a job that you've applied for and really want to get. And maybe you can remember a feeling of certainty, like when you know that you're right about something and no matter how much anyone argues with you or tells you you're wrong, you know with absolute certainty that you're right? Can you remember all those feelings? Did you ever have something happen, like an emergency where you had to act now without even really giving yourself time to think, just do it, get on with it, right now, take the required action and just do it.

Weight Loss - Enhancing Self-Belief.

Amateur- This is a useful script to use once the client is sticking to a healthy eating plan but needs some belief that their efforts are worthwhile and are having an impact on their health and long-term weight loss.

As you continue to rest deeper and deeper, there now, I'd like to shift your awareness deep down inside of yourself, to the place where you store all beliefs and certainties and all absolute knowledge. Some of these beliefs and certainties are about yourself, for yourself, others may be beliefs that others have about you or beliefs you have about others, or the environment you live in. For example I'm sure you have a belief, a knowledge, an absolute certainty about your name, the colour of your car, or that the sun will rise in the morning.

Our beliefs often interpret to our mind and our body, the abilities we have - the things we know we can or can't do. If we had a strong belief that we can walk, talk or drive then our mind and our body allow this to be possible. But if we believe that we cannot do or achieve something then we probably cannot do it. If we think to ourselves I can't do the splits or remember all these things or lose weight then we put ourselves in the wrong state of mind to ever achieve it, even if we have made all of the correct preparations - <u>you must know now that it is true,</u> in order for it to be able to <u>happen now.</u>

A friend of mine spent years trying to <u>lose weight</u> only to find that each time she would either remain the same size and weight, or even get bigger. It didn't even matter if she would <u>eat really healthy food</u> or go <u>to the gym and get plenty of exercise.</u> The weight remained the same because her belief was that <u>losing weight</u> was never <u>easy to achieve.</u> We worked together for quite some time and I was able to <u>talk directly to the subconscious mind</u> in order to say "<u>yes you can lose weight, you will, you can be completely certain of that</u> and you will <u>do it safely and easily</u> within your desired time to achieve<u> it.</u> And we discovered that the real problem had never been that she had trouble <u>stay(ing) on track with the diet</u> but that she believed she wouldn't <u>stay on track with the diet</u> and that was how it was happening. So I said to her whilst in a really deeply relaxed state, probably much deeper than you are experiencing right now, I said "go down into the inner self and find something which gives the feeling of self belief, perhaps something that you know about yourself that is absolutely true - you can be sure of it. And when you are experiencing that feeling I'd like you to be aware of where it starts, how it grows, which way it seems to travel within you, and if it had a colour, what the colour would be.

Now repeat in your mind, whatever it is about yourself that you definitely know is true (and make it nice and positive) repeat it 5 times to yourself in your mind, and each time you say it notice the feeling of self certainty, where it starts, how it grows, which way it travels and the colour of it, and as you do that I'll just take the time to remind you of the commitment you have to achieving your goal and how easily you will do this, adopting this new healthy lifestyle, and looking and feeling so good that it motivates you to continue and to enjoy the healthier options you are taking.

Now that you have focused on that feeling of self-belief I'd like you to apply this to the phrase "I am completely committed to losing weight and feeling great! And say to yourself 5 times <u>being sure</u> to make the sure the colour is bright and travelling through you with definition and as you do that I'll just take the time to remind you of the commitment you have to achieving your goal and how easily you will do this by adopting this new healthy lifestyle and looking and feeling so good that it motivates you to continue and enjoy the healthier options you are taking."

And she was pleasantly surprised to discover that her attitude had changed dramatically. She said to me: "Coming off track is no longer an option; it is not acceptable, only achieving is acceptable.

And you can use that same absolute certainty to commit yourself to achieving with the highest level of self-belief possible to you now. And when people talk to you about your weight loss you no longer say "I am <u>trying</u> to lose weight," you simply say "I am losing weight" because the more you believe that is happening, the more it happens, and the more it happens, the more you believe it and you quickly realise in your general approach to life that whether you think you can or whether you think you can't you'll always be right; so believe that you can and achieve all that you desire.

Appreciating Weight Loss

Amateur - This script is great for reminding the client that a setback is not a failure, but a signal to do something differently. Ask the client by what date they wish to achieve their desired weight before you begin.

Throughout this session you can take time to look back, reflect on how far you have come since the very first time you arrived here. This is something that you can do with <u>immense pride and self-satisfaction</u>. Even though there have been times when it seemed so difficult to achieve, sometimes even setbacks, you have kept going because in your heart, in the very fibre of you that is your own self worth, you know that this task, although it is not undertaken lightly, <u>is achievable,</u> and will create for you, the you, you wish to be, the you that will be, the slimmer, fitter, healthier you.

You can be assured also that by working for this and achieving this yourself, for yourself will be a treasure far greater than anyone could ever give you. Things are appreciated a whole lot more when you have worked for them. For example a young man who wins a million pounds on the lottery may think that all of his dreams have come true, and for a short time at least, this is the case. However, it is often found that a sudden and dramatic change of lifestyle such as this can be quite damaging in the long term as the young man has no time to adjust to his new lifestyle, no support and doesn't value the win and eventually spends all one million he had won. The man who worked every day, concentrated and focused on his goal and eventually made his million, knows the real value of this money. It is his to enjoy, to be proud of, he has worked for it and he appreciates everything he has.

So you can know that too, yes, you will have to work to achieve your goal but this will be something you enjoy doing for very good reasons. Firstly you can look to the future every day to see the new slimmer you and feel confident that you are moving into that image more and more every day. Secondly you can take great pride in saying to yourself and others <u>I did this,</u> I worked for this, this is my wonderful achievement and people will see this achievement in you, every time they look at you. <u>And you remember this every time you think about eating food that will not aid the weight loss.</u> Every time you go to eat something that will not help your diet you think to yourself: you could eat this now *or* you can look like you want to look by (*desired date*). Which is it going to be? And of course every time you <u>will choose</u> the image you will achieve, so you <u>choose the healthier eating option</u> too. And you find that you enjoy and love the healthier food because it is not only much better for your body, but is also much more tasty and nutritious for you.

And if you should ever find - and it will rarely happen - if, <u>not</u>

at all - that there is an increase in your weight or you eat the wrong things one day, you take this as a sign to work and monitor more, not to give up, never give up, never ever. Not until you are exactly where you want to be. You no longer have to say to yourself "you can do it" you can say "I am doing it" and you can feel inside of yourself exactly what it is like to be really achieving. You can feel it in you now and it will grow every day.

Further Weight Loss

Amateur - This script helps the client to focus on healthy food and provides some leverage to help them avoid unwanted foods such as sweet and fatty foods.

From now on you will not use food as an excuse to pass the time or provide you with comfort of any kind. Food is not a substitute for love, activity or anything else it may have been used for in the past. You eat to live you do not live to eat. You eat only when you are hungry and only at a regular mealtime. There is no reason to snack. Snacking only feeds you with calories which lead to fat, snacking is not a means of achieving satisfaction. The only thing food should be used to satisfy is hunger, so from now on, you will only eat at mealtimes when you are feeling really hungry, and then you can really enjoy your healthy food.

This fresh healthy food of many creative tastes, colours and varieties can be enjoyed at regular, well spaced intervals throughout the day. You will find that you must spend much more time planning your meals beforehand, so that you can be sure to be feeding yourself with a healthy balanced diet. This is something you can find great pleasure in doing as you know that you will have so much more energy, enjoying that lighter feeling and eventually beginning to see the decrease in your shape and size.

You may even find that as part of your diligent dietary preparation, that you can be glad to take a salad or fruit snack with you when you go to work, so that you are able to easily refuse the greasy fatty or sugary foods that may be tempting to you as you are working. You can eat your fresh and healthy food and know that not only is it making you feel better, as others are chomping away on their fatty foods and becoming slow and sluggish, but that you are actually making yourself look better, slimmer and more attractive, preparing to bare your well toned body on your next summer holiday.

From now on, everything you eat is good food for you; if it is not, then you do not eat it. You begin forgetting to eat certain foods because they are not in the best interests of the health and shape of your body. You no longer want or enjoy the taste of sugar and as such, it is unnecessary to your body. From now on, sweet foods such as cakes, ice cream, chocolate, sweet fizzy drinks and biscuits will taste sweeter and sicklier as soon as your tongue touches them. Remember that awful furry feeling on your teeth when you eat too much sugar and how too sweet it can taste, as if your whole mouth is filled up with syrup. You no longer enjoy sweet food and drinks, cakes, chocolate, sweets and biscuits can be far too sweet tasting. Imagine now a cake that you would once have enjoyed and as you look at it imagine that furry feeling on your teeth and a strong syrup taste in your mouth as if it is full up with extra sweet syrup. Now you really do not want to eat that cake.

From now on, you do not enjoy fatty greasy foods. When you look at chips or crisps you instantly notice the shiny surface of the food caused by the fat. Imagine that fat floating around in your body in globules, unable to be digested and latching onto your insides of your skin making you bigger and flabbier. You really do not want to increase that, you are now concentrating on burning that excess fat away.

Whenever you see or should you taste fatty greasy foods you are reminded of the people who work in the fast food restaurants in contact with that fat every day. They are not consuming it, yet the fat is so shiny and greasy it seems to have invaded their hair, making it limp and causing their faces to become shiny and spotty. They are not even eating the fat and look at the impact it has. You really do not want to be putting that fatty substance into your body. You are now rejecting all rubbish and focus only on what is good and natural for your body.

This makes you look and feel so much better, you begin to notice the changes immediately in your attitude and motivation and then in your well being and then your size and shape.

Ensure you praise and acknowledge your positive decisions. You do not need to feel as if you are missing out on anything by avoiding certain foods, you are only missing out on getting fatter and you do not really want to do that anyway. You can spend the time that you used to spend snacking, on visualising the way you would really like to look. Take a few moments to do this now and in doing so; you begin to train your mind to accept this image as your new reality.

Weight Loss - Subconscious Protection.

Amateur - This script is useful when a client believes that their weight problems are linked to a problem from the past but are not sure how, why, or even what the problem is that is having an impact on their weight now. This script also contains a resolution for a parts issue, which is a technique used in Neuro Linguistic Programming. During this script the client is asked to communicate using finger movements. Ensure that the clients hands are free and visible before you begin this session

Continue to rest comfortably there, I would like to discuss with you the phenomenon that is your own complex mind. You know that your mind is made up of 2 parts - a conscious and a subconscious (or unconscious) which have different skills and uses. Your conscious mind rationalises questions, and problem solves whilst your unconscious mind works continuously, facilitating your automatic functions such as breathing, blinking and storing away memories.

Sometimes it is possible to be aware of something that you desire to achieve consciously and to experience difficulty in your success because your subconscious has a different agenda to that of your conscious mind. Know now that everything your subconscious mind does, it does with positive intention. Even if it appears problematic or as if it is rebelling against something that you consciously know to be something you must change or achieve. Your subconscious mind will always try to protect you.

However, that is not to say that it is not possible to make positive changes within the subconscious mind, it can be changed to work with your conscious mind to give you the best success in whatever it is that you are achieving.

The trick is to do so in a way that will not offend your subconscious. As human beings, our conscious mind gives us a distinctive skill of curiosity. We want to know why and how about anything that we take interest in and especially about the things which affect our personal feelings. It's funny to think that we know more about the surface of the moon than we know about our own inner minds! But what I can tell you is this - whilst your conscious mind may believe that the solution to a problem is to find its origin, your unconscious mind may try to protect you from that origin if it believes that it would cause you more harm than good to recover the thoughts or memories associated with it. The changes can and will be made, but what you may have to accept is that you may not ever have a conscious explanation for why you have found something difficult in the past that is then changed in the future. And you can find peace in this if you accept that the reason why you don't know the things that you can't know is to keep you safe and happy. And your future happiness need only depend on what you achieve from today and into your future and not from a thought, memory or incident from the past.

And so now change, as I speak to you, you will have both

conscious and unconscious understanding of these matters which have great importance to you. Go deep inside of yourself and become very relaxed and sensitive. I want you to ask yourself inwardly to become aware of the part that controls your eating habits and ability to maintain weight-loss. You may be aware of it as a feeling, picture, a colour, sound or perhaps a slight shifting in tension. Relax as you say inwardly to yourself "Will the part of me responsible for my eating habits and for maintaining my weight-loss make itself consciously known to me." (PAUSE and WATCH.)

You need to clarify that the part responsible for your eating habits is happy to communicate. Ask it to repeat the feelings as a 'yes' signal if it is happy to communicate. (PAUSE and WATCH.)

Signal to me by moving your finger if you were aware of any sensitivity, tension or sensation, colours, pictures or sounds to indicate that you have identified that part of you responsible for eating and maintaining weight-loss.

It is important that you thank this part for all it has done to protect you in the past. Explain to it now that it is important to make the changes and achievements you are aware of in your conscious mind. (PAUSE.)

Ask this part of you if it would be willing to try a new approach whereby it still protects you, but without the negative effect on your weight. Go inside and ask now "Are you willing to try a approach whereby I am still protected but without the negative effect on my weight?" and settle as you identify the answer - a 'yes' answer being signalled in the same way as before. (PAUSE.)

If the answer is yes, ask it to make the necessary changes to adopt its new approach now, if no sensation was received then that means that it could not identify any suitable strategy to adjust to. If this is the case or if you found that your approach was accepted but that aspects of it may need altering, please ask the part responsible for eating habits to now go to the creative part of your subconscious and ask it to create many new ways that it knows <u>would be acceptable</u> in providing protection without any negative effects on your weight, allowing you to lose weight easily and maintain your target weight. Ask now and await its quick response.

Ask it if it feels that your creative mind has made 3 acceptable strategies of the many it created, then ask the part if it would be willing to try any of these new strategies. (PAUSE.)

If the signal is yes then check that all aspects of it are acceptable using your creative part to create new ones if they are not, and then make an agreement about when the change of strategy will begin. Do all of this within your own mind, right now.

If you need to find more strategies or approaches you can continue to do so as I speak, so either continue to make those inward changes or <u>rest as I speak</u>. Because I suppose that one thing that could really hold you back here is if you make all of these changes but do not consciously <u>believe that they have occurred</u>. And because weight doesn't simply fall off over-night, you could've spend many months doubting the credibility of the fantastic work <u>you are doing</u>. Then in a few weeks time just as the difference really begins to start showing, you would have convinced yourself that it was all a load of rubbish and it is always so much easier and more comfortable to slip back into these old damaging beliefs.

So what you <u>will do</u> instead is accept the reasons I have given you about why it is important to not know about certain things and how it is that you've changed them anyway, even though they are gone. Now let all of those parts become one force that can help you progress and evolve. You can be re-integrated as a whole. And you can still be protected by <u>something... is now significantly different</u> in that you can diet and enjoy dieting, you can find it really easy to eat healthy natural foods - and enjoy exercising and walking and dancing - with each breath feeding your energy - and you can propel yourself away from the figure of the past to a comfortable figure in the future as <u>you tell yourself positive things</u> - you notice <u>you feel more positive and you start to feel better</u> - life gets better and when you hear that critical inner voice <u>stop... yourself and find a more encouraging and constructive way to deal with the problems</u> - and speak to yourself in a friendlier way. Because what you believe you will achieve. So believe this when I tell you this is true and most importantly believe in yourself and <u>accept that</u> you have made that change and notice what a difference it makes - look out for the changes, that increase in energy returning to you now.

Weight Loss - Change Personal History.

Professional - This script asks the client to communicate with you using their fingers throughout their trance, so you will need to ensure that their hands are in a comfortable and visible place. Using this script with your client allows them to have the opportunity to make changes to the way they view their unsuccessful attempts at losing weight in the past.

And as you <u>continue to relax deeper</u> I want to completely reinforce in you the power you have over your own life, your own destiny, and your ability to achieve, successfully, your desired weight in the desired time. To be sure that there is no chance that this task will be sabotaged, I want to take you back to the very first time you experienced an unsuccessful attempt to lose weight. Perhaps there was one particular incident, comment or trigger that wobbled your confidence in your own ability to continue with your weight-loss. It may be something you are completely unaware of that has affected your perception in all further attempts to lose weight. Whatever it is, will be found and eradicated so that you no longer have to fight against it, there will just be you and your determination to succeed and flow.

Firstly I would like you to remember the most recent time that you experienced a lack of confidence in your ability to lose weight, and signal by raising a finger when you have recovered this most recent memory.

Remember where you were, what you were doing, who was with you, notice if anything was said or done by you or anyone else to cause this reaction in your body and mind.

I want you to be there with that image of yourself in that situation, and I want you to offer that younger you, in that situation some kind and encouraging words. Talk to that past self and give them the self-belief that they lack, really mean it, really make him/her believe it. Tell them they can do this and give them all the encouragement they need to succeed. Tell him/her why he/she mustn't give up, why he/she mustn't sabotage her/his efforts. Perhaps you will need to offer some comfort or wise words to change the way he/she is feeling. You can offer a different perspective to his/her thinking to change their feelings and behaviour. Now I want you to grab that past other self by the shoulders, look into his/her eyes and tell him/her "You can do this." and don't just say it, mean it, feel it and believe it, right down in the very fibre of your being, believe it and tell him/her that he/she really can and really will. And when you are satisfied that you have given that belief successfully to never give up, never ever, I want you to move back to the bridge of time to the next event in your life where you gave up or lost hope. Again go to that image of yourself: *(Repeat the paragraph for the next event.)*

I'm going to give you a few minutes to continue travelling to other significant times, repairing and reassuring, making the necessary changes, offering advice and comfort until you have corrected every situation, every reason where you gave up or sabotaged your efforts. When you have done this (take your time to do it completely) then please indicate that you are finished by raising your finger.

Now I want you to imagine a situation in the future where you may be tempted to stray, or give up - and if you can even do this - then I want you to step into that picture, step into yourself and say "stop" and coach yourself the way you have in all of the past situations giving yourself all of those reasons to remain committed and focused. Do that now and when you have done it once, do it again, if you can *even manage* to imagine another situation where you might stray or give up, then step into that situation and into yourself and say "stop!" and give yourself all of the encouragement you need, all of the reasons to focus on success and do not stop until you have successfully convinced yourself that <u>you can and will achieve your goal.</u>

And now you have created in yourself a very useful tool that you can easily use for yourself. Knowing that a real achievement peaks and occasionally, gently troughs. Before hitting the target even a dart that is destined for the bull's-eye trembles and wobbles somewhat as it cuts through the air, never direct in its journey - and that's ok. It's fine to sometimes make blunders or under achieve because when you look back on how far you have come, you've done so well and you're so certain about the target you will hit, you keep flying, full power until you reach the bull's-eye.

Split Road Weight Loss

Professional - When we have options we have power over the choices we make and this can give a great sense of empowerment. This script gives two choices about how a client can progress with their attitude to weight loss.

Now as you <u>become more comfortable</u>, I wonder if you can remember how <u>easily and deeply you entered into relaxed trance state</u> before where there is only the sound of my voice and your understanding as you become more and more relaxed with that consciousness of your own <u>unconscious</u> mind.

Nothing troubles you as you prepare to work the powers of your subconscious mind to help you now move on from your problem of the past, that bothersome thing, knowing that here within, there...you really do have the answer, the solution, <u>so</u>

<u>relax</u> as I continue to speak to you. I want you to imagine that you are standing in a peaceful place upon a road.

There is a road behind you. This represents the life you have already had and the experiences you have had in this life. Ahead of you the road splits, going in two different directions. One direction represents a healthy life, a life of healthy food, exercise and a healthy body. You see that this road slopes uphill slightly and this is because to take this path requires work and effort. But you see that the road is pleasant, well lit and bright with the sweet sound of nature.

The other direction is a flat road, much easier path to take. However the air is thick along this path and it looks dark, dreary and isolated. As you look from the past to the future you can clearly see the transition from familiar to unfamiliar territory. You know that both of these paths are meant for your steps only. You know that one path is a healthy path and contains hints and guidelines for your confidence and well being. Allow yourself to be completely open to this. The other path is a sickness path. It is best represented in this way - the feeling of total intensity, the weight on your body, breathlessness. I want you to consider for a moment the quality of life you might experience on each path, the people you might meet. The way you would look.

Begin first with the sickness path. (PAUSE for 2 minutes)

Now I would like you to spend some time experiencing the healthy path. (PAUSE for 2 minutes)

The paths show you that you have moved on from the past, and have options about the future. I know that <u>you will choose the healthy path</u> because you have already made your decision to do so that is why you are here. Stare ahead now at this healthy path you will take, where you can start to enjoy a new life, enjoying everything around you. Enjoying being alive, feeling really good to be alive with a calm peaceful mind. Relaxed, at ease, living with respect at being alive, and enjoying every phase of it. Determining from today that you will make your life as good as you possibly can in every way. Being aware of how good it is to move and exercise and be active. Knowing with absolute confidence and certainty that you will be no longer be left behind because of levels of fitness or weight.

How good it is to be physically powerful and healthy and how wonderful to swim, walk and run and to also breathe as easily as you are now. Starting today it can feel so good when you keep fit, so good to eat healthily. When you move, when you walk. You're going to feel good to control your thoughts and to feel how good it is to be physically powerful and healthy. And you'll amplify the quantity of exercise, of effort, of walking, of moving, it will feel really good as you become more and more alive. You'll begin to enjoy everything more, like a child who is full of energy and never stops moving and you can be very happy to be alive.

Exploring Food

Amateur - Use this script for those who do not enjoy or avoid eating healthy foods.

It's time to start looking at new ways of doing things, to explore new horizons. Sometimes this can seem daunting at first, the unknown is often thought of as something to be feared, but you've been an explorer your whole life, often without caution, without even thinking about it - and this is the best way to discover new things about yourself.

Do you remember your first experience of being on a beach barefoot - the sand beneath your feet, warm and grainy underfoot, and the feeling of it moving under and around you as you paddled in the cool sea? Perhaps you later had your first taste of sweet wispy candy floss.

Or perhaps you remember exploring snow. Laying in it, touching it, tasting it, observing it closely to see if each individual flake really is unique - staring straight up to the sky and watching the snow drift down towards your face from high, high up in the clouded sky.

Or perhaps you can remember the very first rainbow you ever saw and wondered if there really was a pot of gold at the end of it - did you look at the way the colours integrated into each other?

You can remember that exploring new things is fun and easy to do and that the only thing standing between you and the pleasurable exploration experiences is your false presumptions that you will not enjoy trying new things and altering bad habits.

Perhaps, before exploring as babies do with their ability to taste and explore with their tongues and mouths, you might consider, as you peel an orange, the waxy skin - now even the zest is considered edible in sweet marmalade, removing the soft white pith before separating each individual segment. And have you ever noticed how within each individual segment are hundreds of little pods filled with sweet juice?

You may have noticed that there is a star running through the centre of every apple, if you find the right way to cut it.

But looking and observing fresh fruit and vegetables may not be the right way for you. Perhaps you enjoy discovering aromas, noticing the subtle sweetness, delicate sourness, warm woody undertones, or soft feelings, smooth, prickly, lumpy and the bumpy.

You might find it much easier to discover the fresh fruits and vegetables of which you have no expectations - no knowledge - like wiping the slate clean and say to yourself "This might be the food that I'll really enjoy." And in the naivety of new experience, discover refreshingly that you can really enjoy, salivate, swallow and feel satisfied.

You might even find more faith, trust and confidence in your ability to change and grow, as you explore your interest in growing fresh fruit and vegetables of your own. Watching them change and develop, tending to them lovingly nurturing them with good light and food and water, caring for them with the love and respect you show your own body.

Weight Loss Getting Leverage.

Amateur - Use this script on its own or in conjunction with another weight loss script.

Now you and I both know that a certain kind of desire, of motivation is required to <u>make all of this work</u>, and perhaps that is a little something of what you have, and perhaps you need much more to make your money and both of our time worthwhile.

And <u>it is up to you to *do this*</u>, when <u>you choose to stop treating your body like dispensable dumping ground.</u> But you know that your body won't put up with it forever - it's already giving you the warning signs - your tummy is a sign that your lifestyle is very unhealthy for you. Which sign will you wait for next?

We've all experienced the loss of someone we love or something or a situation we value - and we can be aware of that loss from our lives. You can be aware now of the responsibilities that you have towards those that love and care for you, close people who rely on you to be there for them. The responsibility that is yours and yours alone to ensure that those people will not be faced with the loss of a person whom they treasure and love, your responsibility to ensure that you are there for them that you live a long and healthy life, respect and protect your body, appreciating your gift of life, that person eating only what's good for you. Eating foods which are healthy in the right amount at the right time. Not so much of that man made rubbish and more of the natural foods of the earth.

But I know nobody likes to be told what to do, so I won't say that overeating or eating fatty greasy foods is dangerous for you. That they are dangerous and prevent you from having the body you desire Slim and firm and beautiful.

I will not tell you that fried and sweet foods are so high in fat and calories that you will get <u>no</u> pleasure whatsoever from eating them. I would not tell you that, I would instead ask you to simply think of how you will look and feel differently as a result of making the healthy choices you will now be making.

~

Quit Smoking Scripts

~

The Ultimate and Approved Quit Smoking Script
By Gemma Bailey, Karen Hastings and Adeline Munoz
Professional - This script touches on most aspects involved in smoking. Remember to find out what age the client wants to live until during your consultation.

You've taken the step that will free you from being at the mercy of a bad habit. There is no need to feel ashamed anymore. Those disgusting smells and tastes will no longer be a part of you. So just lay back and relax, more now. You can find that you can just drift here and there, listening and not listening; it's up to you to do this. Either way, changes are being made. Because you have made this commitment to create a healthy reward for yourself, so reward yourself now.

You can feel proud and confident that you will achieve this with ease. Perhaps you could begin to <u>feel this now</u> and allow those feelings to increase throughout the rest of this session. Always drifting deeper and deeper.

I want you to know that throughout this process you will feel safe and secure. You can <u>quiet your thoughts and only listen to the sound of my voice</u>, so that I can guide you to the deepest level of trance. If anything pops into your mind, notice it and <u>let it go.</u>

You've come to the right place, here, now. And it won't be the first or last time that you find something easy. Perhaps you're here because you may have noticed that you find it difficult to shake off a cold or that you get out of breath sooner than you'd liked.

Of course smoking accelerates aging, robbing your skin of oxygen and nutrients, causing you to look old and grey....do you want this?

Yellow teeth, yellow fingers, lines above the upper lip, the smell that's followed you like a shadow, until you made the decision, to <u>STOP NOW,</u> and starting to breath better now.

You said you want to live until you're _____ in order for that to be realistic, you need to start taking responsibility for your health and the health of those you poison with your filthy smoke. Because....you can do this easily. .. you <u>can</u> take that responsibility. After all, life is for living, and living is life.

Ammonia, usually washed around your toilet basin, for cleaning away germs and urine...I know that you know that strong smell. Benzene from petrol, made to fuel your car, not to fuel your body. Formaldehyde used for embalming the dead...but you're not dead yet. It's quite something that you have been inhaling these chemicals into your body eagerly.

Tar deposits lining your rattling airways. Carbon monoxide kills when it is breathed in. When you breath it in, you are killing many things...inside you've been deliberately inhaling it.

Now I'd like to say that this is something you haven't been doing, but you have to admit you <u>have</u> been <u>doing this to yourself</u>.

As everyone knows, you have been foolish. You bought into the lie/bullshit, that smoking helps you to relax. Does it? That it de-stresses you, that it is sociable, that it makes you more confident, or that can think more clearly...what is clear, is that smoking does none of these things for you. You have been lying to yourself. Now is the time to be honest with your selfish disregard for own your health and life.

I know that you know that smoking has been damaging you. It has never saved you, but now is the time to save yourself. People can be in control without smoking. Knowing that you can as you relax and go deeper.

I am curious, how have you managed to deny cancer all this time? A smoker is 50% more likely to create cancer, within their own body. Cancer causes suffering, pain and loss, it invades and spreads. How would you feel, sitting with your family, having to tell them that you have ignored the warnings and could be gone long before your time?

It's selfish to expect those people who rely on you to be part of their lives to forgive you for what you have inflicted. Feel the shame and guilt, and know that you are ready to say goodbye to these feelings.

You have caused a war within yourself. Be at peace now, in every cell. Stopping smoking isn't a battle for you, you can be victorious.

I will now be silent for 2 minutes whilst you spend some time observing yourself in all those old situations where you used to smoke, now seeing yourself in these situations without cigarettes; it's simple to find that you can. Notice how easy and natural it feels to observe this behaviour. Clean and new. Next time you hear my voice you will have made the transition, if you haven't already done so. I will spend the 2 minutes' silence considering all of those who have lost their lives due to smoking.

(2 minute silence)

The changes have been made. You can be curious about the difference you feel... may be slight or even bigger and it's great that you are... a non smoker can feel proud now, accepting that this new belief in yourself may be slight but will grow with each day and each and every cigarette you for get to think about.

And what you will notice is that by now, your blood pressure and pulse have returned to normal. As you continue, by tomorrow your oxygen levels will have regulated themselves. Carbon monoxide and nicotine will have cleared and vanished forever within the next two days. By _____ (day in 3 days time) You're breathing ... will be easier and your blood will flow strongly... freely, giving you energy. I know that you will easily and naturally refrain from smoking for 9 healthy months so that you can clearly enjoy the benefits of improved quality, breathing and strong cleaner lungs. When this happens, you will then feel more certain that you will never smoke again.

With all your new energy, you can enjoy the increased benefits of healthy exercise and outdoor activities (with family.) You can be aware that you will only put health and goodness inside your body from now on. Your skin is becoming clearer and smoother and your grey pallor is replaced with warm hues. A sense of freedom embraces you now, more calmer and relaxed, realise that smoking really was a false friend that only served to help you achieve illness and stress.You are naturally drawn towards healthy choices about what you do and don't put into your body. Replacing smoking with only healthy alternatives which enable you to feel freedom from the guilt you used to have. Knowing that you will be there for those you love and care about…living.

And just think… about all of those thing and experiences you will be able to spend your extra money on, sleeping better at night.

Your senses are flourishing. Taste buds experience an explosion of flavour, you smell delicate fragrances like never before. Tasting and smelling everything in the finest detail. Seeing clearly, your mind is now able to focus, no longer clouded by a dirty fog. Your appetite for living a healthy life….

Should you ever smoke again in the future, you're unconscious…will remind you in instantly recognizable way of your commitment to yourself and those that you love. If you ever put a cigarette to your lips again, you will instantly suffer from the cough that you have worked so hard avoid, burning at the back of your throat, light headedness causing you to feel nauseous and unwell. The wasted effort in being here today and remaining a non-smoker for all of that time.

Knowing now, that you can be around people who smoke, feeling pity for them and have no need to smoke, knowing that you can finish a meal and have no need to smoke, knowing now that you can work with pressure and have no need to smoke, knowing now that you can go where ever you want, whenever you want for however long you want and having no need to smoke.

Stop Smoking Metaphor- That Foolish Man

By Gemma Bailey, Karen Hastings and Adeline Munoz

Amateur - We created this script using the Dreamweaver Process. For greater power it is best used in conjunction with another quit smoking script.

Perhaps you know the story of that foolish man? Most people know the story, but do not want to understand it, I wonder if you can? He was a happy healthy man, as people are in the beginning, lulled into temptation by the lapping waves, offering their false gift. It won't be the first or last time that gift is offered. People don't consider the implications. For what appeared to be a message in a glass green bottle, was in fact a map on stained yellowed paper, a map that would lead him to a deadly treasure.

Of course, upon finding the map, he is instantly filled with a mixture of emotions, as he remembers the legend, traditionally told of those who had perished in the company of the treasure, never to return. Considering the qualities that the treasure may offer, he ponders. Noticing this, the lapping waves, as if reading his mind almost seemed to gently whisper to him, encouraging him to begin.

After a brief investigation, he is surprised at how easily he finds the treasure at the back of the cave. Unusual sounds reverberate off the stone walls, seeming to come from nowhere and everywhere. Feeling concerned, with each and every footstep he takes, murmurs and echoes seem to implore him to turn back. Perhaps it was someone who loves you, who told you to stop and turn back? Still he continued.

There's a stench. Staleness pervades the air, so that he can almost taste it, dirty air. His eyes have difficulty adjusting to the darkness, but they eventually do, and he notices a silky red cloth covering a box of sorts. Could this red cloth be a warning? He does not question. He tears and peels back the cloth, as he does; a cloud of filthy dust explodes into the air, choking him into fits of coughs, covering his face and the insides of his nostrils with a dry grime. Wiping the dust from his eyes, he sees the treasure, glowing misleadingly.

This glow lightens the cave only enough for him to recognize the skeletons around him, cant you? Immediately, he realises the truth disguised within the treasure and vows to free himself of this fate. But every time he tries to leave, he fears what will happen if he should leave. Will he be the same without the treasure? He assumes he can't cope. I mean, do you already know someone that has?

For a long time he is drawn back to it, whenever he tries to leave, growing stuffy and stale within. The air of decay is around. He grows weaker in each and every cell. His skin beginning to grey and age, but still he is invaded by the obsession of the treasure.

Unsure of how much time has passed, he grows lonely and ashamed, seeing others happy and healthy, he is not, enjoying their lives in the sun.

As the cave grows darker, he becomes desperate to leave and calls out for support, commanding someone to hear his cry. Responding, a member of a ship's crew, comes to the entrance of the cave and holds up his lantern.

This illumination of the cave, gives him the ability to see clearly. He draws in a deep breath at the sight of the treasure, now visible as a can of worms, squirming and sliming. Repulsed by the reality of all he has wasted, he quickly moves away with ease and certainty, stepping out of the cave, into the clean fresh air.

As the sun rises his cells are reforming, he is growing strong and healthy, his mind is free in the knowledge that he will never return to that dark place. And now he can enjoy the earth in all its beauty.

Quit Smoking Confidence

Amateur - This script gives suggestions for disregarding any cravings that the body may have after giving up smoking. This is particularly useful if the client has quit smoking before and has had cravings or is concerned about having cravings after quitting via hypnotherapy.

I know that you've had first hand experience of the negative impact of smoking - the breathing problems - I mean something as ordinary and easy and automatic as breathing suddenly being an effort, hard work.

The constant rattling chest and coughing, the weakness and the damage on the inside that you cannot even see. Just imagine if the people that you'd love and lost from smoking were still here now happy and healthy.

Yet they chose to let a stupid addiction to a little white stick take them before their time. I'm sure for you; you would be greatly missed by those that love and care about you - yet what example are you setting - what children in your life see you as a smoking wheezy and weak person, when in your mind there is still so much to achieve in life.

Perhaps it's time to make the decision to *not* end your life prematurely as you have witnessed others do; but to remember how ill it has made you, and vow now to give it up for good and begin to live your life in a whole new clean and fresh way. And immediately you will feel better, life will become easier. You will be free again to relax comfortably and deeply, breathing in only clean fresh air, purifying and healing your body and filling you with energy.

After just a few moments of becoming a non-smoker, or perhaps now, you will be completely happy and confident without cigarettes, in fact, each time you think of cigarettes the memory only serves to remind you of how ill they caused you to be, and this is such a frustrating thing that you will eventually decide to stop thinking about them altogether.

You will instead find time to do many productive and energetic things. At first, your body might take a few days to detox from the years of abuse from these nasty old cigarettes, but after a while it will blossom, just like the garden. I want you to treat your body just as you would your garden - put only the most beautiful things in, help it to be healthy and free of parasites, make sure you care for it. Then the plants will grow strong and much life will exist there. Every day in every way you will become stronger and fitter and with more energy, every day in every way. I know that there are challenges in life, big ones and little ones. I know you have had some experience of both and if you think now of a big challenge that you've overcome in the past, you'll see that giving up smoking was nothing compared to that big challenge - and when you recognise how easily you overcame that big challenge, you recognise how very simple it was to be giving up smoking - didn't you?

You are very strong, you know your own mind and your mind says "no more smoking" and when your mind says something as confidently and with as much certainty as that, you'd better pay attention because ultimately your mind is in charge. There might be times when your body thinks it's in charge and it claims to want this or want that, but really it would do well to listen to the mind, because the mind will always be correct, not the body, and if you just stop and listen to the mind you will know it is right to just stop. The body is a bit slower at adjusting but you need to let that happen so that it can and then very quickly it will. Then it will start to tell you "I want something else. I want to relax in the clean fresh air" or "I want to do some exercise" and your brain will say "That is a good idea, yes I think we should do those things" and when you will, you'll find yourself so pleasantly surprised at how easy those deep breaths relax you, just sitting there and enjoying the nature of it all. You'll be even more surprised at how confident and certain you are feeling about the fact that you're actually going to stop smoking and enjoy it.

You're going to feel great, fit and fresh and clean as if you've just come to the earth and noticed many new and wonderful things. Everything healthier- healthy in all areas only good things into your body now.

Cigarettes and Alcohol

Amateur - This script is for those who want to quit smoking and moderate their alcohol intake and for those who smoke when drinking alcohol

Everyone likes to relax; and it's great to know that <u>you can,</u> in easy and natural ways, either on your own or whilst enjoying others company also. And you can do this, as a perfectly normal thing to do. You can chill out and have fun and you don't need anything to help you achieve this, you've been doing it your whole life via your magnetic and wonderful personality.

Now I know that, as much as you like to relax and have fun, you also take great importance and pride in your health and body. Without these, there would be no fun. So let's be serious for a moment. When we drink alcohol, something about us feels indestructible, powerful even. And perhaps, coupled with that, you've convinced yourself that smoking makes you feel more confident, sexy or that it is sociable. In your mind, you know that smoking really does none of these things for you. It does not serve you in any way.

So I wonder now, what are the many ways in which you have ignored the dangers of smoking...whilst you are drinking or perhaps you have chosen to simply ignore the many dangers? Do I really need to remind you of the cancers, asthma, and emphysema? The suffering, the loss. Of course, I do not need to insult your intelligence - you already know what can happen to you if you continue with this.

A friend of mine had a step-brother whose cousin used to smoke whilst drinking. One night, he had a little too much to drink, and with that, smoked *a lot* too much. He was shouting about over the noise of a party, singing along to songs, smoking and drinking. Toward the end of the evening, his voice became more and more hoarse, uncomfortable, even. He went to bed that night with the dirt and filth in his pipes, his nose blocked, his clothed and body stinking and he passed out.

In the morning when he awoke, his wife asked him about his evening out. But when he tried to answer her, no sound came out of his mouth. His voice had seized up completely. He felt as if he were talking properly, as there was no pain, just a little tightness, but no sound at all. He went to the doctors and was prescribed antibiotics and to rest his voice. Do you know how difficult that is? To rest your voice. Unable to speak at work, on the phone, when ordering lunch or requesting a train ticket. To lose your voice, to have no say....how terribly frustrating. Can you image how your life would be, if you couldn't be heard?

It was at that point that he said "<u>enough is enough</u>." And he stopped. He could still have a drink and have a good time and from time to time he even thought about smoking, then he remembered what that would cost him...long term... what is it costing you?

You can drink and have a good time, and know that you are still responsible for taking care of yourself. That you still have a body that needs to be taken care of.

Cigarettes and alcohol. Sounds very rock and roll doesn't it? Yet did you know that cigarettes and alcohol is an anagram of "scatological adherent." Scatology is the study of faeces. Adherent means enthusiast. Surely that tells you something about cigarettes and alcohol and what you are putting into your body. Next time you drink and feel keen to smoke, you truly can remember that you're being enthusiastic about filling your body with yet more crap. And perhaps, you'll begin to feel differently now about being in control of your own thoughts and actions.

Smokers Relapse Script

Professional - Use this script when a client has had some success after using hypnosis to quit smoking, but has been tempted to re-start. It incorporates an NLP technique called a Swish pattern which is useful for creating new neurological pathways.

I'm sure; <u>now</u> there is a part of you that feels a sense of profound disappointment. Having firmly made a commitment, a promise to yourself for your own health and wellbeing. Your future good, and that of your family, who you love and care for, and who love and care for you.

You did achieve - committed to your promise and confident in your task you set about achieving, <u>moving forward into your future life as a non-smoker</u>. And you enjoyed the freedom it gave you, the feeling of feeling better, freer, healthier, no longer hiding a dirty secret. Yes, you had to overcome the habit, the addiction, but <u>your confidence in yourself, your ability</u> allowed this to be possible.

However, due to pressure or perhaps childish impulse you decided to have a cigarette.

If you thought that you could have only one then you were wrong, however, if you consciously decided to begin your old habit then you are just plain foolish and wasting both our time. I ask that at this point your subconscious mind listen carefully. <u>Your eyes will remain closed</u> only if <u>you genuinely wish to stop smoking for good</u>, never to start again. If you should now find that your eyes have opened then this is a signal from your unconscious mind that you do not wish to stop smoking for good, make this decision now. *(Wait a few moments to see how they react)*

Thank you. *(If their eyes have opened, terminate the session and explain that you will need to do some extra work with them to provide further leverage.)*

Ok. I understand from your subconscious mind that <u>you have committed to stopping smoking forever</u>, no longer burdened by the impulse to smoke and confident in your ability to live life free of a dirty destructive habit.

So all that is left for me to say on the subject, since you have already made the decision to stop completely forever, without my further intervention is to ask you to focus on 2 different images.

I need not give lots of vivid description about these as your creative imagination is able to assist you fully in this and you have after all, already decided to stop smoking. So in a sense all this task is doing is ensuring that you are confident in your decision and to make sure you feel as though you've got your money's worth from the original session you attended.

Firstly, picture on the screen in your mind a picture of yourself as a non-smoker, confident, clean, happy, healthy. Not smoking in the car, clean and fresh in the house and at work. Picture your family, continuing to be proud of your achievement. Look at how much better and happier you seem. Relaxed and controlled. Now move that picture to the bottom right hand corner on the screen and in the large space remaining, fill it with a picture or image of yourself looking desperate, pathetically in need of a choking, dirty cigarette, using the last few pennies of your hard earned cash to struggle to buy a packet. Imagine now that you are indulging in a dirty secret cigarette one evening at home and your (family member), increasingly suspicious of the vile smell around you, catches you smoking. Now, I can't see the disappointment on his/her face. But I imagine that it's far worse than any momentary satisfaction you ever gained from a cigarette. It's probably enough to put you off cigarettes for the rest of your life, so that is the choice you make - give up cigarettes for the rest of your life, and when you have made that decision, slowly begin to drain the colour out of that old smoking image and if there is any sound with that old smoking image, turn down the volume and alter the tone. Distort the image of smoking so that it no longer has any value to you.

Then, as I say swish, swish it away and replace it with the

picture of the non-smoker that <u>you are, confident,</u> completely free and happy. Ready SWISH eliminating all short term pleasure smoking gave you Swishing the smoker away completely. *(It is a good idea to repeat the Swish process several times.)*

Now I would like you to go back to the time when you most recently experienced complete confidence in yourself as a non-smoker. I want you to feel yourself actually back there, experience the feeling of confidence at a whole new high. Now, we're going to go back over the bridge of time to retrieve that feeling of confidence and instil it as a permanent fixture in your very being, to remain forever in every fibre of your body.

5 going gently back into your feeling.... Over the bridge, back through time, 4 through the fog, curious to discover and excited at the prospect of experiencing that confidence permanently. Knowing that <u>you belong, as a non-smoker</u>.

3 the fog becoming less dense, as you begin to notice shapes and colours, things that represent your highest time of confidence to you, 2 everything seems much clearer, 1 and as that image of complete confidence moves towards you, surrounds and envelopes you, at my next count, allow it to fill your soul, breathe it in, for you to accept that total confidence now, at 0.

And when you are certain that you have achieved that state of complete confidence, follow me back over the bridge of time, <u>leaving the fog and smoke behind you.</u> Much more aware of any snares that anybody, even you, may set for yourself by tempting you inconsiderately with a cigarette just to see <u>how easy you find it to resist them</u>. Now that you have complete confidence in yourself, you can be confident that the hypnosis has and always will work.

~

Self Development

~

Hurt in Love

Professional - This script helps to desensitize the client from the negative emotions they are experiencing using elements of the NLP fast phobia cure.

Now you can become more comfortable. You can become more and more at rest and at ease, more confident with each phrase, each word that I utter, as it will all make so much good sense. So much more clarity will occur that your mind will be open to my suggestions and will act upon the messages it hears.

We are going to move through time, from the past to the future and we are going to look very carefully at how events and situations can be viewed in a way that will make you feel much, much better about who you are and everything you have to offer.

I know that there are certain unwanted emotions that you have been dealing with recently and it is important that you realise the power of your emotions and how quickly and easily you can make them change. Have you ever watched a movie and experienced a multitude of emotions for the characters you are watching - happiness, fear, sadness - and that all occurs in just a couple of hours.

So you can be sure of the speed of change in your emotions that we can create in the time that we have together now, some very positive work will be done.

I know that the bad feelings you have experienced lately all stems from unfortunate events in the past, when you felt your whole life was turned upside down.

A person, with whom you had shared love and trust, suddenly extinguished the value of that love and trust, someone with whom you thought had created security, pulled the rug from under your feet. I know that you were really hurt, so I do not want you to re-imagine it, just consider these thoughts:

You have an innocent gift of love and it would have served no purpose for you to know the workings of your lost love's innermost mind and I will tell you why. If (s)he had wanted to change or feel differently about something (s)he would have sought your help. (S)he did not. There was nothing you could do to prevent it so you are getting yourself organised, you are seeking help to help yourself feel better, growing stronger in yourself, more sure of yourself, you are in control of you. You are not broken, it ended this way and (s)he did you a favour, you see her/him now for what (s)he is and the relationship for what it was.

Now, knowing all of that, keeping that in mind, I want you to see yourself in front of a movie screen, not looking through your own eyes there, for you are in the projection box above, looking down at yourself, sat comfortably in the cinema, waiting for the movie to start, And the *(name of client)* in the cinema looks really calm and confident. Now this is what I want you to do, put on an old black and white movie of the day *(client's ex partners name)* called you to end your relationship. It's in black and white and the sound is a little distorted and as you play it watch it from the projection box and also watch *(client's name)* sat there in that row watching the movie, and you will see that (s)he remains quite calm and still, (s)he has no emotional reaction to this film. Put the film in the projector and press play and as I count from one to five relax and go deeper and play the film throughout my count, starting now 1,2,3,4,5.

You look down from the projection box and see that *(client's name)* in the cinema is still calm, emotionless about the movie s/he has seen. Now I will count quickly from 5-1 and as I do so I want you to watch that movie again, backwards, in black and white, very fast. You will notice that the voices sound a bit odd, a bit silly going backwards and fast and high pitched as you watch the film backwards, very fast in black and white as I count begin now 5,4,3,2,1. And as you look down at *(client's name)* in the cinema, you notice that (s)he has a lighter look about him/her, perhaps it's because of the silly voices in that old black and white movie.

Now, float down out of that projection box into your body, in the cinema and look through your own eyes up at the screen. You have in your lap, a remote control, so again play the movie in black and white of the day *(client's ex partners name)* called you to end your relationship. Watch it quicker this time, paced with my count of 5 and you will notice that the faster you go, the higher and more ridiculous *(client's ex partners name)* voice sounds on the phone. Begin now 1,2,3,4,5. And as you begin to notice the insignificance of the old movie I want you to listen to it and watch it again backwards back to the start as I count backwards. Ready 5,4,3,2,1 *(count fast)*. And in black and white all the time play forwards now 1,2,3,4,5, and backwards sounding really silly now 5,4,3,2,1, desensitising you from that situation forwards 1,2,3,4,5 and backwards 5,4,3,2,1. Feeling new, clear, lighter and refreshed. From this moment onwards you are in complete control of your feelings and emotions. And what of the future for *(client's name)*? It is time to think about leaving the cocoon of sorrow to emerge as a beautiful butterfly, so take good care of yourself and make yourself attractive, be beautiful and there will be plenty of people longing to be near you like bees around a honey pot. And spend your time thinking beautiful thoughts about those who are worthy of your thinking energy. You will not waste any more time on wondering after people who are not at all wonderful for you. And you will love and trust and rebuild yourself <u>far more robust than before</u>, taking your time to develop lasting relationships in the future. Repairing, no longer a soul of destruction, you will not let him/her take anymore of you because <u>you are stronger than that, far stronger</u>. It may not always be the most comfortable feeling to be in new places, getting on by yourself, making new friends but you find that the more you do this the easier it becomes and the more you become a strong person with more and greater opportunities than before.

In fact, <u>this will take so much of your time</u> that you will not have time to consider being alone. You will find that your intuition increases and that you have far more confidence in it from now on. When you look back, emotionless at those situations where your intuition told you you were right or that something was wrong, you know now that it really was so. You no longer doubt yourself. You were right to feel those uncomfortable feelings but you never needed to change the things about yourself that others can love, you are entitled to much more love than that.

You let go of feelings of shame or regret - you are not guilty of anything. You can feel proud at your inner strength in reaction to what has happened to you. You know now that there is no doubt, that you are not guilty of anything but doing your finest. You were then, and you are now being the finest person that you can be.

Each day is offering you a new beginning and you can <u>create your life brand new</u>. Yesterday has gone. You cannot live in the past - otherwise you'll be stuck there. Your past only equals your future if you spend your time in the now, thinking about the past and living in the past dulls the edges of living. Of course the past can help you to learn and be better in the future, such as the inner strength you will nurture now. Looking at what has gone hides from you what you actually have. A better future, no longer volatile. Look at what you are and who you will become and take great pleasure from those things. And there is no time to regret, had you have not had the experience of being with that person you would have regretted never trying and never knowing, so regret is not of any use here. You can be thankful for this experience.

I'm going to be quiet now and leave you for a while so that you can make peace within yourself. Allowing the power of your own inner mind to do its best work for you. When you are satisfied that you have done all that you can comfortably and safely do here, then you may gently wake yourself with a feeling of excitement and contentment that the future is there waiting for you to make it your own.

Living with Narcissists

Amateur - use this script when the client has people around them who are always pointing out their failings. It will encourage the client to focus more on their own strengths and disregard the doubts of others.

It's funny, isn't it when you think back to those days learning every day at school. How at that time it seemed to be important to do well at absolutely everything. People, parents, teachers seemed to believe that each individual should have equal abilities in each area to make us well-rounded, equal.

Either poor in all subjects, or average or good or outstanding in all subjects. When really people are not like that. Generally, people have preferences and greater abilities in one subject or another. Some are more creative and less articulate, some are more sporty, yet numerically challenged. You understand what I mean. So is the answer to keep pushing and punishing for the things we don't do well or don't enjoy. Should we keep looking at our lesser abilities and keep trying to improve them?

That is what most people do and it makes them feel bad - if you're wired in a way to not be so great at art, or not very good at sports then why trouble yourself about it, why put yourself in those situations that you know will be unpleasant for you? It doesn't work, and if what you're doing doesn't work you should do something else.

So here's my tip: Do more of what you love, get really good at, excel at, what you do well. Re-discover your finest qualities and nurture them only then will you be true to yourself, happy and appreciate yourself for who you really are. And you'll find that all of the other stuff, the stuff that other people expected from you, that you and they made so much fuss about, really was not that important, well perhaps it's important to them, but you don't have to share their worries, let them keep them.

If you ever want to take on other people's worries and problems, make sure they're paying you for it.

It's only when <u>you have made the decision to live your life in a different way</u> and <u>feel better about yourself</u> that you become aware of the need for boundaries - the kind of emotional protection that we need in order to have self respect and to earn respect from others. You will see in others, those that have little self respect - it makes them feel out of control and there are only two different things that happen to these people. The first is that they become bullies inflicting physical or emotional pain on others; it makes them feel more in control. You might know some people like that, quite often, they never change because part of their need for self respect is met by getting some control when they hurt or upset others.

The other thing that can happen to people when they have no self respect, is that they spend a large part of their lives getting hurt over and over again. You might know someone like this. The reason why they consistently go back and interact with the person that hurts them (or feel drawn to) a variety of people who all hurt them in the same kind of way is this: having pain, is better than nothing at all. Having nothing is like death, and you can feel fortunate to know that somebody loves enough and is interested in you enough, to cause you pain, it would be worse if they were to ignore you completely. Now the really good news is this, there are 2 very simple things that this kind of person can do to change. The first is, <u>love yourself</u>. Spend time learning new things, setting yourself goals and feeling good when <u>you achieve them</u>.

Despite everything, you can feel so proud of who you are and who you will be. The other thing you <u>must</u> do, is to spend time with the people you want to be like. So make friends with people who <u>have</u> self-respect and boundaries. You won't have to try to do what they do, the change will happen automatically, I'm sure you can think of people you know with negative characteristics that you've unconsciously adopted, the same thing will happen when you spend time with those positive characteristics.

So you have some important tasks, discover what you are good at, embrace your good emotional qualities, recognise them and get really good at the things you love.

Recognise your weaknesses and <u>then focus on what's great about you</u>, rather than feeling bad about who or what you are not.

Set your goals and praise yourself on your achievements, spend time with the people you would want to become. And lastly, do as much as you can <u>now</u> to <u>enjoy now.</u>

There is <u>only now</u>, the past is gone, it has no benefit to continuously recreate it, the things you fantasise about in the future will only ever happen if you put them into action in the <u>now.</u>

Now I'd like you to remember everything we have discussed and later today, or perhaps right now. Think of all the excuses you have to not <u>do all of the useful and empowering things I have told you to do</u>. Then take each excuse, examine it closely and put it in a bin in your mind which is used especially to dispose of silly excuses. Remember that your past is just history, yet your future is a mystery and the present is a gift, it's time to be grateful for it.

Accepting Happiness
Amateur - This script can be used when a client simply needs to change their attitude and focus to enable them to be able to "see" the good around them.

Sometimes in life it can be really difficult to adjust to changes - even if part of ourselves knows that <u>it is for the better</u>, we are more comfortable with the old situations - even if it is not healthy or profitable - it is at least what we know and are used to.

Attitudes and mindsets can be the same. I know so many people caught in a trap of negative thinking who are terrified to think positively - for fear that something positive might actually happen to them!

And then they would feel differently about everything -

happier with what they have and happier with who they are. And happiness can bring all sorts of amazing troubles - <u>good fortune and feelings of love and self worth</u>. Happiness is a dangerous business! Some believe that they are much safer with bad feelings. They know what to expect - after all they've had them for such a long time they've probably formed quite an attachment.

Well you and I know that <u>you want something new</u>- That's why you're here. To make yourself <u>feel better about yourself</u>. You're going to start making a few changes, sailing closer to the wind of happiness and create a way to <u>get to that feeling, any time you want it.</u>

What your mind can conceive, you can achieve, so throughout this session I want you to be reminded of situations when you have felt really good about yourself and who you are. Perhaps recently you have put pressure on yourself to prove yourself as a constant and consistent success. Well, you already are a success because you're still here despite it all, and I'm sure that there is even better for you to come.

Progression, development and success rarely develop to their full potency under pressure. Relax and be happy. It's time to let yourself grow.

Loss

Professional - This script is ideally used following the death of a friend or relative, but could be adapted to include the loss of situations or objects that are causing the client to feel anxious about further loss in the future.

It's ok to <u>let go now</u>. Time to move forward, the future, it's all new. And you can, in the future, remember those you have lost, but remember too, to enjoy the moment of now. Those you have loved, would want you to, wouldn't they? Enjoy your life<u>, enjoy living it</u>. It can be difficult, sometimes, to lose someone or something we love. Some people can become anxious about loss, yet that is life, it evolves, anything that is lost is replaced, in some way. It keeps going, life goes on and you become stronger.

Perhaps what is lost is not replaced until you find that strength in yourself? Learn to let go, enjoy what you have instead of upsetting yourself over what is lost or what you may be losing. In fact, if you wake up every day, and think of everything you have and everything you have to look forward to you'd probably forget to think about everything you might lose, which you probably won't lose when you're thinking happier thoughts anyway.

There is so much to lose, if you worry about it, you can see it everywhere, but you've been doing this for so long and it's making you unhappy. Now that you can understand what this all stands for, you can let it go. It's ok to let go. It doesn't mean you don't care. It means that you can see the difference and that you're comfortable with yourself, who you are, how you love. You do not need to be afraid of losing, here you always did the best that you could.

And so much more will grow, as a result of your loss, when you choose to see it and accept that sometimes we need to let go, to move forward, it doesn't mean we don't remember, it's just that you're ready now to stop worrying about what's gone, accept it and move forward. Look for everything new that is growing, create it yourself. It's time to move on, don't forget, but let go of what's lost. You are safe and protected here and there are easier ways to deal with and express your loss from the past, without looking for things to lose each day.

If you look, you will always find. Look at all the wonderful things you can gain and create and grow today and tomorrow.

Candida

Amateur - This is a metaphorical script that uses the garden as a representation for the stomach. Using antifungal treatment in the garden, gives the client permission to use their own biochemistry to get the Candida under control.

Now listen carefully. I want you to imagine a beautiful fragranced garden, full of brightly coloured flowers of your favourite kind. I want you to start paying much more attention to this garden. This garden that <u>you are</u> <u>inside now,</u> <u>noticing different things within,</u> <u>as you relax there,</u> this garden <u>you're within,</u> represents your body, the ecosystem <u>inside of you.</u> <u>You are within yourself</u> there. Now, you will see, that on the surface, from a distance, the garden appears to be well kept, maintained, full of colour and beauty. And it is. However, some time ago, deep underground, where no one really thinks about too often, weeds began to form, having had their seeds dropped incidentally and uncaringly by a flying bird who was just trying to get his business organised. The weeds, harmless while in the ground, began to grow and eventually upset the surface by appearing in amongst the neat lawn and flowerbeds.

If you look more closely at the garden as you rest there now, you will see the weeds and the toadstools grow in the lawn on the flowerbeds, and around the base of the large trees, there is a frilly fungus. The weeds and the fungus are now at a stage where they are beginning to damage the flora within your garden. When you look closely you feel that the weeds and fungus have become overgrown. You know that action must be taken to prevent the weeds and fungus reaching the walls of your garden and causing any more damage.

Now I want you to <u>go down</u> the slope behind you, to where the garden reaches back and back and down and back. When <u>you have gone down</u> and back far enough, you will find a gardening shed. It is large and filled with many resources. Using the key which is in your pocket, un-padlock the shed and step inside. There <u>you will find all of the resources you need</u> to remove the weeds and fungus. If you look on the shelves you will find a powder or solution, I'm not sure which, <u>you will know it when you see it</u> - it is an organic antifungal treatment, there's plenty of it there. Take it and put it into a watering can, which you will find beside the door. There is an outdoor tap attached to the garden wall, you need to add plenty of water. Now, leave the watering can to one side, and go to the back of the shed.

On the far wall is a blueprint of the garden in perfect health, the only way it should be, the way it is when it is just full of healthy flora. As you become familiar with the blueprint, I want you to recall where it was within in the garden that you saw the weeds and fungus and you will soon realise which areas must receive the organic antifungal treatment, which is safe to use in all areas of your garden.

When you know where to start I want you to find a biodegradable sack and a pair of gloves from the shed and take it with your watering can to the most affected part of the garden. Don't worry if the antifungal treatment spills from the watering can, it is perfectly safe and there is plenty of it. Walk slowly- I know the can is heavy. Now when you reach the right place, set down the can and put on your gloves. Now do you want to open the sack and see just how much of those weeds and fungus you can clear with your own efforts just by being in a healthy way, always using encouraging, healthy language as you work, putting the weeds and fungus into the sack. It's funny looking at it now, these little weeds, little rots were just trying to take over your garden, but when you take control, you find you can remove them quite easily, you move around the garden, removing all of the weeds and fungus and rubbish in all areas of your life. When you see the weeds and fungus as insignificant, that is exactly what they are.

Now when you are finished, I want you to check the entire garden to make sure all of the weeds and fungus have been removed. Check the walls, the joints, the flowers, the sinuses, the trees, the organs, the pond and the body tissue. When all of the surfaces are clear, tie up your biodegradable sack, with all of the unwanted rubbish inside and take the sack to your natural waste disposable unit, from which place it can leave the garden clear and healthy. Now return to where you left the watering can full of organic antifungal bacteria and sprinkle each area generously, the lawn, the flowerbeds, the base of the trees . . . . .to dissolve the underground network and roots of the weeds and funguses on and under all surfaces.

There will of course be a small amount of fungus that lives on, it is always around in every one of us, but you are now able to tend to your garden, to be in control of it, encouraging the flora to grow by only feeding your garden with the correct kind of vegetation. Return the gloves and empty can to the shed, back down the slope, back and down, back and down. Put the watering can and gloves away and take another look at the blueprint on the back wall. You may notice how it seems to look that much bigger and brighter and more colourful than it did earlier. You can help to achieve this brighter state by replenishing the garden with only the most beneficial and nutritious plants that grow into health and energy and well-being.

So find some seeds and plants from your shed to take into the garden now. And as you walk back, enjoying the newness of the future, you can decide upon the best places for your flowers and seeds, then gently place them into the damp soil. As you are planting, there arrives a soft warm rain, cleaning and cleansing, helping everything to settle and drink more water. As you tend to your garden, from now on, the seeds begin to germinate and grow, replacing the lost fungus with health and well-being and energy. You can see it all happening, even as you return to re-padlock the shed, you can hear yourself thinking in a much more positive way. Feeling much more focused on the good things that will occur in the future. Candida exists in all of us, but from now on you pretend it isn't there. Candida can indeed get better.

Body Returning to Good Health

Amateur - This script encourages the client to utilise their own inner thoughts and language to help repair their body.

When you look in the mirror, what do you see? Is this the real you, or just another created thought that will prompt your subconscious to deliver a pre-programmed perception of you, a product of past experiences and conditioning? Well, whatever the answer to that question may be, and you may need to think really deeply about the answer, I want you to know that how you see yourself is going to change for the better, to improve your quality of life, to cleanse and refresh you, like a gentle cool breeze, blowing away the cobwebs that have masked your beauty and abilities. So that the confidence you have in yourself is able to grow and develop, stronger and stronger, every minute, of every hour, of every day.

Now let us begin by first focusing on your body. Your body is an amazing miracle of nature. How many plants and trees do you know of that are able to affect their health just by thinking positively? And how many animals do you know that self heal with the power of their minds? Yet you have the ability to affect every part of your body, simply by thinking about it, you can make yourself better. This is called getting what you focus on. Have you ever thought of buying a new car and suddenly you start to see the car you are thinking of buying being driven around everywhere! It's the same sort of thing. Only when something isn't going well, it's not enough to think "I don't want this illness anymore . . ." or "I want to stop worrying about my ailments . . ." because your perfect intelligent mind will focus on what you have said, irrespective of whether you want more of it or not. This can result in your mind thinking "I want this illness." and "I want to worry." From now on, I want you to start to review and sensor all of the thoughts in your head and all of the language from your mouth.

And focus on the positives that you want to achieve. So every day you will say to yourself "My body is returning to natural health" and "My body takes care of me. I can relax."

There are so many functions and skills that your body commands without you even consciously realising it. Your blinking and walking and talking are all automatic and I suspect that should you decide to think about these too much, these natural, normal functions may begin to seem quite odd and unfamiliar. And I imagine that the more you concentrate on that oddness and unfamiliar-ness, the more uneasy and concerned you could become quite stressed in these parts of your body. Let's focus on the fact that your body is automatically rejuvenating itself, and it does this best of all when you relax. And the more you relax the better you feel and the better your body performs its natural functions.

So during next week, I want you to forget to think about any problems you may have <u>with your body relaxing</u> and <u>focus on feeling well</u>, you'll be amazed at how much <u>better you feel</u>.

Organisation

Amateur - This script can be used for those who have a list of things to do and do not know where to start.

Can you imagine how life would be without the numbers and letters and symbols we've come to rely on? How disorganised everything would be. Never knowing what to do, what instructions to follow at which time. If there were no yesterday, tomorrow, now….. It all makes little sense without order, it needs sequencing, organising. <u>You need to start doing things one at a time</u>. Only then can you <u>decide what goes next</u>, or what went before or what you must do now. And when <u>you have completed, one after the other,</u> then the next, until it is all in order, it will all be so clear. <u>You can see what was and what is</u>. It will be so much more peaceful, clear, space and time. <u>It's so easy when you put things in order</u>, and weightless once the tasks are completed. It can seem daunting, even starting on the chaos of bits and pieces, here and there, this and that. And the more you try to ignore it and pretend it isn't there, the more the chaos and mess grows, the more you see it and the more it bothers you.

Now, it will get to the point where you just cannot bear to put up with the disorganisation of it any longer and that <u>frustration will give you the energy to start rapid and consistent structure</u>, in all areas of your life that you identify as needing organisation. Now the decision to start this restructuring and reorganisation of each area of your life, your home, may begin in sequence, first this, then that, or perhaps a couple of sudden spurts of energy, just to get everything organised. Now that structuring and organisation might occur in an hour or two when you arrive home, or perhaps tomorrow. But <u>you know that it will occur in some ordinance</u>, somewhere between now and then, and after it happens you will experience such relief, such satisfaction, such joy.

A lightness, lists ticked, you can feel the difference, no longer burdened by the invisible pressure weighted by waiting for your own motivation to arrive. You can see the difference, look at how much clearer your surroundings will be when you have that control, it is all within your reach. And how that will make a difference to you, you'll actually look different. And when you listen, hear peace. No more nagging inside to start this and finish that. Just satisfied that you have enough organised, you have been productive and structure this day.

<u>Now it is clear in your mind, you must make it clear all around you</u>, and then there is peace.

Because you can see, life works so much better with a little organisation and sequence. Numbers, letters, symbols, instructions, time after time. Now and tomorrow, now and the next day and the next, from now into the next month, the next year and all of the future, one day after the next, following sequence, it's all in order now.

Positive thinking for exams

Amateur - This script is particularly useful for children and young people who have exams coming up. This script also uses an NLP anchoring technique which you will need to explain to your client in advance of using this script, and also ensure that they relax with their hands in an accessible position.

I remember a time when I had to do a whole load of exams at school, and they were the kind of thing that I generally am quite calm and relaxed about; I don't get too excited about these things.

With these particular exams, it was a bit different; a strange and curious thing began to happen. The nearer it got to the exams, the more and more my teachers began talking about them, quite intensely, and my friends seemed to be clucking away talking about them like a coup of nervous chickens. And it was as if the exam fever spread around like measles, infecting everyone, eventually including me, until just the word "EXAM" on its own could stir up uncomfortable feelings inside. I mean, let's face it the word exam doesn't seem to have a very pleasant meaning to it. So here's what I did. I banned the word exam, and I changed it to a new word, a less intimidating word, a less scary word.

And me and all my friends stopped using the word exam and instead we used a different word. A word that created a completely different set of feelings inside, some more relaxed feelings shall we say, feelings that even made us smile. Instead of calling them exams we called them boggies. And we'd get to school on exam day and say "How many boggies do you have today?" "Oh 3 boggies today, a small art boggie, an English boggie (cos of course you can get French boggies) and a massive maths boggie. I'm looking forward to my maths boggie but my art boggie could be a bit sticky."

And when we had to think about which subjects we wanted to do the following year, we all sat and had a giggle about picking our boggies. And the funniest thing happened. Because we'd all relaxed and stayed calm, we all did surprisingly well in our exams (boggies!) You see the thing is, nobody's ever going to ask you to choose between the red wire and the blue wire. It doesn't matter how important the exam is, you're not disposing of a bomb. You don't have to choose between the blue wire and the red wire, the future of mankind doesn't depend on you, it's just a boggie.

And the great thing is, that you only get questions that you already know the answer to. It's all within your ability to achieve. And did you know that 40% of answers in an exam appear somewhere else within the paper? So here's what you're going to do. I want you to <u>remember a time in the past when you felt really confident</u>, really good about yourself, it could be any time at all. And I want you to remember that time now as if you were back there seeing it through your own eyes, hearing what you heard and feeling how you felt. As you feel those wonderful feelings once again I want you to squeeze your fingers together especially when you're feeling really good:

Repeat for the following states:
Confidence
Ideas flowing
Found something easy
Happy.

Now what I want you to do is create a movie screen in your mind and on that screen I want you to play a movie of a few days before an exam. You're at school/college and notice how everyone is behaving; perhaps they look a little bit anxious. <u>Now see yourself in the picture looking calm and normal, focused on doing really well in these exams, really easily, really confidently and extremely calmly.</u> You know that the *(client's name)* in this movie is staying calm and saying encouraging things to her/himself like "you can do it easily; you know the answers you can be certain of that." Now see yourself later that evening, revising for the exam

74

tomorrow. See how easily *(client's name)* seems to absorb the information like a sponge, then access it as quickly as a rugby player about to score a winning try in the world cup. S/he's happy that s/he knows everything s/he needs to know so s/he chills out listening to some hypnosis to give her/him an extra confidence boost so that s/he's sure <u>you can do it easily</u>. Now fast forward the movie to the exam, see *(client's name)* calm and relaxed, enjoying his/her boggie oops, I mean exam! Now notice how when s/he gets to a question s/he's not too sure about, s/he makes a note of the question number, because s/he's extremely keen to solve that problem easily and the answer will probably pop into his/her mind as s/he continues getting on with the other questions, so s/he can go back and fill it out when s/he remembers all of the answers simply and calmly completing all of the test confidently and in good time. Now fast forward to the end of the movie where *(client's name)* is getting the results of the exam. This is the first time s/he if feeling that fluttery feeling inside and that's because s/he knows s/he did really well and is excited about hearing just how well s/he did.

Now step into that movie and see through your own eyes, hear through your own ears as you find out that you are top of the class. Now feel in your body how it feels to have done so very well done and how proud you are of yourself, so much so that you can't wait to tell everyone and see the joy in their faces. Now squeeze your fingers together at the peak of that feeling of pride and happiness.

And whenever you want to experience all of those good feelings in the future, you only have to squeeze your fingers again to enjoy them.

You <u>(client's name)</u> are <u>a very clever person</u>. You know exactly the right things to do and say and how to behave to get the results you want. With your determination to prove to these whoever dared to doubt you (how dare they) <u>you excel and succeed every time, in everything that you do.</u>

Certainty for Public Speaking Presentations

Amateur - Use this script for a client who has a specific public speaking presentation to make.

Certainty, it's a funny thing to describe, because when <u>you have it, you know you have it.</u> A sureness, a knowing, knowing that <u>you know with certainty</u>. A confidence within. And there are things that <u>you know, you know,</u> and things that you don't know that you know, but <u>you know them all the same,</u> so all that is required is to be certain of all of the wonderful abilities that you have, to drift and dream, relax and go deeper, to make things happen the way you really want them to happen, to be the master of your own destiny.

<u>There are things that you already know</u> that create certainty within you - perhaps you are certain of your own name, or that the sun will rise in the morning - you might not be able to see it behind the clouds - but it will be there, <u>you can be certain</u> of it. So the sun will rise, and so will you, preparing yourself in a calm and confident way, automatically following your normal morning routine, paying particular attention to <u>your presentation which will feel and appear relaxed and confident. Giving a relaxed and confident presentation, as easily as relaxing right now.</u>

<u>And you feel, as you look at your reflection in the mirror that your presentation will be very good,</u> very confidently presented, as confident, as sure as the sun will rise in the morning. And as your reflection stares back at you, you <u>see a well prepared, interesting person, someone with a motivation</u> to set the record straight, say her/his piece, make her/his feelings known, share the knowledge and the truth. You are your own best friend, a knowledgeable and well resourced individual, and you speak to yourself, <u>inside,</u> in only the same way that you would comfort and reassure and encourage a best friend who is going to overcome her/his fear and present herself/himself perfectly, <u>a perfect presentation.</u>

On your journey there, be there now, seeing what you will see, hearing what you will hear, saying what you will say to the others around you, if there are others there, feeling your clothes against your skin, <u>rehearsing in your mind</u>. And as you travel, or arrive and wait or at anytime where all you are doing is going inside of yourself and imagining your presentation and how it will be when the time comes to do it, if at any time you start to feel those old feelings of anxiety, then this is what I want you to do, and you can do this now, here, in the safety of hypnosis.

Firstly, allow that initial anxiety <u>that excitement</u> - that anticipation of what is to come. Take the picture that you make in your mind, that big picture up there and this is what I want you to do with it - move it lower down, further away, put the colour in black and white and alter any sounds/voices you hear as a result of that picture.

You could make them squeaky or ridiculous sounding. If you can then, even manage to create the same tension as you used to feel, then I would just like you to remember the most relaxing experience you have had recently and to remember every part of that relaxing experience - where you were, <u>how you were breathing</u>, how you were thinking and feeling. Do that now.

And if you can even remember how you used to do those anxious physical symptoms, then I'd like you to take that feeling that would have rushed from your head downwards and as it moves downwards, move it right back up again and as it moves up, deep breath in, your shoulder straighten, head up, and feel clarity and certainty. Now, when the time comes for you to present yourself, you say to yourself "I can do this, I will do this" you will believe this because you are certain it is true, you have practised this in your mind, <u>you are as certain about this as you are certain that the sun will rise in the morning.</u>

When all of this will be over, after all, your life will go on and these moments are only a small fraction of your entire life - the sun will rise tomorrow, and today you will shine. When <u>you can</u>

do this, you can do anything and you can do this. So you take - to your stand. Composed, articulate, accurate, steady and sure you confidently look at those who address you and take a deep breath before answering each question. And you think to yourself "I'm doing so well!" Suddenly the questions become faster, more fired, more accusing - you sense a flutter beginning in your chest.

Will it grow? No. You are in control.

You take a slow breath in, enjoying the pause; clear your throat, relaxed and confident. Speak clearly, composed and articulate, surprised at how relaxed you feel, how easily you react, how vividly you recall.

As you finish, you step down, but remain feeling high - after all what an achievement! You can reward yourself with an encouraging internal "well-done." Your task completed, simply and easily, the most testing presentation passed with flying colours.

You can enjoy the satisfaction of your achievement and even begin to look forward to your next public speaking scenario.

Everything happens for a reason and the reason is this: your future holds many amazing opportunities that are yours for the taking, some you may already know about, others you are not yet aware of, but you can be certain that there is an interesting and exciting future waiting for you - things that you have the capabilities to do now, that you were not capable of doing before, and if you do not trust yourself then no one else will. Tomorrow the sun will rise, even if you cannot see it, but from today and everyday from now you will shine.

Control Without Controlling

Amateur - This script encourages the client to take responsibility for their goals and actions to give them a greater sense of control, and to also recognise that some things are best left to others.

I know that you know the importance of having a purpose in life. Achieving your goals helps you to grow and it's important to grow.

A friend of mine went to a seminar which was presented by Tony Robbins. He said,

"Everything in the universe is either growing or dying.

And in order that you grow you must keep achieving your goals and desires. It's a good idea to visualise in your mind all of the things you most wish for, why what are dreams for if not to come true? What some people tend to do instead is to dream about all of the things that could go wrong. This only causes upset and frustration; it causes them to feel out of control. Being in control is about imagining what you want and then doing it. Most people imagine what they don't want and complain when they get it. That's a good example of how to feel out of control. Control is knowing what you want and getting it. Some people have a misjudgement about what control is. Realistically there are very few things in life that we actually can control. We can control our decisions, our thinking, our feelings and our reactions. However we cannot control other people, the laws of the universe or the weather. If we could control everything, after all, life would be far too predictable.

So it's important to understand that we can control only ourselves and hope that the others we interact with have similar ideas, values and beliefs about where they are going in life that fit in with your own. So for now just relax, because I know that you know what it is that you want and where it is that you are going and I'm certain you'll achieve it. And you can be flexible enough to make allowances for any obstacles you might encounter on your way. You can be flexible enough to overcome them easily. You are resourceful enough to get yourself to where you want to be, whatever it takes to get you there. Because you know exactly what it is that you want and you take control of yourself to get it. You have taken control of your life before, been able to make good things come of challenging situations. By taking control and going for what you want you achieve good. <u>You make yourself happy</u> and that makes others happy too. <u>You have your own best interests at heart</u> and have always done the right thing; you can continue to do the right thing for yourself in the healthiest possible way. Having control is about having certainty and drive to achieve that wish you are certain of. It's a bit like having faith.

I recently went on holiday to Egypt. Egypt is a very curious place - full of magic and mystery. One night we sat in the desert and looked up at the stars. If you think that you see the stars in the countryside then that's nothing. The sky in the desert is filled with millions of sparkling stars and ablaze with them shooting in all directions. <u>You could imagine</u> the chariots racing across the sands moving someone of great importance to where they needed to be. Back towards to the great holy pyramid to guard the Rosetta stone. The future key to the understanding of those ancient times, because it's good to have communication that can be clearly understood by those to whom you are communicating. Can you imagine the detail and work that went into building a pyramid? First they probably had a very clear idea of what they were hoping to achieve, they knew their outcome. Then, someone had to take control of the project, someone who knew exactly what was wanted. If there was anyone within the project who didn't pull their weight or didn't have complete commitment to see it through to the completion, then they let that person go, and probably carried on without them for a while, with everyone else doing a bit extra, until someone else came along to assist with the completion of that project.

They had faith that what they wanted was achievable and worthwhile and everyone had to be on board to make it work and that meant that someone had to take responsibility for <u>driving the project forward</u>. You can understand how having

someone take control is very important. It can be done gracefully, in a relaxed way and with diplomacy." He said

Shopping Cessation

*Amateur - this script allows the client to experience the excitement and
wonder of shopping whilst in a trance. The end of the script contains
embedded commands to prevent them from shopping so much in the
future.*

Just <u>drop right down now</u>. Do you remember <u>drifting and
dreaming</u> in a place where there was only <u>peace and calm and
quiet</u>?

Move lower to that place now and wherever you go, you will
hear my voice. My voice can even echo throughout the left and
right of your mind ....going back and back .....

Have you ever dreamed, with total clarity? And although you
know, it's just a dream, you feel all of the emotions, as if it were
real, it's as if <u>you are really there right now</u>, and you see things
and hear things as if you were right there, revisiting a special
place from long, long ago....As you look down at a cobbled
pathway, with crunchy white snow falling around your feet, you
can see your shoes and as you lift your head, your hands in gloves
and coat, and the clouds of your breath as it hits the air.

In the distance is the sound of a horse pulling a carriage along
the street, people chattering, doors opening and closing. The air
is cold and damp against your skin as the snowflakes, large like
feathers continue to fall gently. As you look down the streets you
see lots of little shops and boutiques, warmly lit and elegantly
displaying their vast interesting and expensive goods. Old-
fashioned lamps laden the pavements and those who pass you
are smartly dressed and talking busily. As you head now, <u>down
the street</u>, your shoes crunching in the snow beneath you,
<u>relaxing deeper with every step</u>, creating lightness, easiness
within you.

To your left a door opens with the jingle of a bell and warm air meets the side of your face. Head towards the shop where it is warmer, I cannot tell you what is inside as the windows have steamed slightly, so you will need to go and find out, and you really want to know, so step in and feel the warm air on your face and hands, causing your fingers to tingle as they make the transition in temperature, and around you, are hundreds of candles, so many shapes and colours and varieties, filling the room with flickering warm light and sweet smells. Lavender and vanilla and chocolate to name but a few, you gaze for a moment, watching an increasing pool of wax collecting at the wick of a huge church-like candle, slowly, drifting to the edge before melting gently down, overflowing its warm liquid and collecting and solidifying at the base of this slowly melting candle. Relaxing you as you watch the flame flickering at the wick, blue and yellow and orange dancing light.

You need not spend a long time in here; take a deep breath, inhaling those warm sweet smells once more before pulling the door which jingles the bell again and stepping back out into the crunchy snow which is still drifting down. As the door behind you sinks back into its wooden frame, head further down the street, if your hands feel cold, sink them into your pockets, deep, deep down into the warmth there. It's easy to leave with money in your pocket.

The next doorway has a window lit with tiny lights that appear to be moving and as you draw cautiously nearer, notice how they are like tiny stars, not like anything you've ever seen before, they seem to be alive, and moving in synchronicity with each other, it's as if they're playing there like dancing fairies, quite remarkable. As you lift your hand toward the door they dart away from you, causing the light to lower as you enter the shop. When you step inside, you stamp the collected snow from your shoes upon the deep, dark rich carpet and look up at a vast collection of clothing and materials. Reach out and touch something on a rail, perhaps a smooth silk, almost liquid in texture or leaf through to a soft velour in royal blue, or a rich velvet in racing green. If you go down the rails, the metal hangers squeaking as they move, perhaps you will find something that you'd like to purchase, there's some money in your pocket, anything you wish for.....or perhaps <u>you will not buy</u>...

When you are ready, leave the shop, step back outside and cross the cobbled road, under a lamp is a bench which has been kept dry and clear. Take a seat and rest your head, just watch the snow falling toward you, sinking down, floating, drifting, until <u>there is nothing else, just you inside your mind</u> and the sky all around and the snow falling down and around. <u>Relaxing you deeper</u> with each floating flake, like feathers, <u>softly, slowly, easily, deeper and deeper</u>. It seems to arrive from nowhere, it doesn't matter, but its pleasant and calming, and although you are alone, you feel safe here, comfortable, drifting all around you. You can return here anytime you wish. <u>You can experience the feelings you used to feel when you were spending money shopping. You can have them here, and later feel no need or desire to go shopping.</u> It's your choice, just watch the snow.

You could spend your money or s<u>now more.</u> It's your choice s<u>now</u> <u>more</u>....shopping. S<u>now</u> <u>more</u>, gently. It's much better to go home with money in your pocket, just think of what you'll be saving.

Driving to success

Amateur - This script is for those about to take a driving test. It enables the client to feel calm and relaxed whilst remaining focused.

<u>Just relax deeply down now</u>, you can be aware of my voice, or you can drift and dream, so that you can just lay back and relax.

Do you remember, as a child... <u>that curious nature,</u> how you used to love to learn, how easily, and quickly you would develop new skills? And you have learned so many thing... <u>you are even</u>

learning now as you rest, your mind is learning even whilst you sleep. And you can surprise yourself at how quickly, simply and methodically that all information can return to you, it's automatic, as if there is a large comprehensive manual stored in your mind, you automatically retrieve that information from that very clever manual.

I know… you know, that at some level, you love to perform, everybody does… to have a few minutes in the limelight, everyone loves to show off their wonderful skills sometimes, to indicate what they are truly perfect at. Smoothly, you pull off of your manual of experiences, automatically, gracefully, when you are in this powerful state you are concentrating in a relaxed way, your reflexes alert and your heart beat steady. You know where to look, in order to get the best possible result. Do you notice how the universe supports you as your memory changes gear enabling you to recall all of those well timed manoeuvres? Yes I know how you love to perform…and in everything, there are times when you need to slow down, always taking it steady and at other times at a moment's notice, you need to stop completely.

Then always pulling gently away…. .moving forward with ease and confidence. You've learned so much and you're driving your knowledge in the right direction now, so that you can use it, you're in the driving seat and it feels great. It feels wonderful to know that you have all of the answers at your finger tips. Wonderful being so comfortable and relaxed and able to concentrate on exactly what you are doing, so that you perform it perfectly, better than your very best practice, practice, practice in your mind and practice engineering your own success.

Which way do you need to go to drive towards success here, left or right or straight on? With every turn of the wheels of achievement you're nearly there, you can wipe away your worries and accelerate towards your dreams you can do anything that is humanly possible, you've been learning and remembering so easily all of your life, without even thinking about how easily you do, so calmly and confidently.

You're breathing...is relaxed, you're not exhausted but well fuelled, full of energy to remain alert and consistent in your efforts. Your mind, like a well oiled machine is seeing everything, functioning in such a way that it's doing so many different things. Keeping you safe, you in your bubble, travelling safely amongst all of those around you. You can see them, be aware of them, of the part that they play, contributing to your experience, and you keep them safe. You keep them safe by knowing where they are and sensibly keeping your attention on what you are doing, where you are going.

You're in control and you control where you are going and how you get there. You're in the driver's seat and loving this performance this drive towards your freedom. You know you can do this, and in this process you enjoy sharing your ability, you're modestly showing off your skills and you feel great doing it.

You've been learning and remembering all of your life, you can do it so easily, it's almost as if you don't even have to think about it. All of the skills are there you're remembering as easily as you remember to breath easily.

Look After Yourself

Amateur - This script is useful for clients who have neglected their health and wellbeing.

This is your time now, for yourself, to look after yourself, to heal and rebuild yourself. Time for you to reorganize quietly in a corner of your mind, all that needs reorganising. Time to let go of any anxieties or worries, becoming free of all of those things that you are unable to control. Realising how to best take care of yourself, look after yourself and create your own happiness.

It sometimes can seem so unlikely, that we are the masters of our own destiny, that we choose how happy or fortunate or successful our lives will be. Imagine, just imagining how happy you want to be can create that happiness. After all, you get what you focus on, so always focus on what you want. Very often people come here to ask for my help, they lay there in that chair all heavy and relaxed and comfortable, just as you are now and I ask them all of the questions that I asked you which can seem so very confusing at times and what tends to happen is, that when I ask them what it is that they really want out of life they start by saying " I don't want to feel like this or I don't want to behave like that and I don't want this happening anymore." And then I have to explain to them that their very intelligent imaginative creative mind is so very sensitive and will always focus so very hard on achieving for you all of the things you are thinking of. So if you are thinking "I don't want to feel like this" then your mind will focus on "feel like this" and you end up with more of the feeling you do not want to have. Or if you are concentrating really hard and thinking "I don't want to behave like that" then your mind will focus on "behave like that" and you end up experiencing the behaviour you wanted to avoid. So you see, it is never about thinking about all of the things you don't want, you must always think of what it is that you do want to see, hear, feel, taste or where it is that you want to be.

And you can do this so easily for yourself, whether it refers to your lifestyle, your relaxation, your situation you can do this easily. And a very useful way to reinforce your ultimate success is to build your self-confidence and acknowledge all that you have achieved so far in what you might have considered to be quite difficult circumstances. You have done so much for others in your life, whether gratefully received or not, you can take pride in your effort, your compassion, everything you have ever done, you have done with positive intension. And this you do whilst overcoming so many difficulties - at times heartbreak or struggle - you have helped so many people in your life.

If you knew someone like you, they would be a true and valuable friend, someone who really shows that they love and care; even if at times they feel that the love has not always been reciprocated. And you would tell that friend that inner self that they have so much more that they haven't even yet begun to use: so much more love, competence, ability to be at ease, to enjoy life, live fully and to look after yourself.

You would give that friend the best possible advice about how to take care of him/herself properly. Perhaps s/he needs to focus on how s/he can maintain his/her wellness by having a healthy diet. You could help him/her to plan and prepare the right things to eat or you could talk to him/her about his/her routine or show him/her how easy it is to relax completely and let go of all of those unnecessary thoughts so that s/he is able to relax and sleep peacefully and deeply.

And when s/he is worried during difficult times you can help him/her to solve his/her problems and ride the wave until the difficult time passes, and it will pass, it will improve. And when s/he notices that you seem to be caught up in your troubles, s/he would do well to remind you that you are not immortal and you do not even know when you will meet your end, so it is important to use the time (which I'm sure there will be plenty of wonderful time) to your very best advantage. Divide it well, some just for yourself and some for those whom you love and care for and who love and care for you. Enjoy every moment of your precious time, for when it has gone, those fleeting seconds can never be retrieved. Never the same experience at the time ever again, so use it wisely.

Freedom of Choice
Amateur - This script will help to encourage a client to look beyond any perceived boundaries in a situation.

Every day you make choices, there is always choice. You know that you have freedom to wear what you like, watch what you want on TV...It's funny, you know I was talking to a friend the other day and she said about how she never votes at elections because she doesn't trust any of the political parties. And it suddenly dawned on me that in some countries the people there would be too afraid to say such a thing - here, we even have freedom of speech and it reminds me to be grateful.

Now, <u>go inside your own inner mind, go back and back</u>, past the relaxed left and right lobes to an ornate spiral stairway with an engraved banister. <u>Go down the steps,</u> travelling towards the part of your mind that most desires to be free. When you reach the bottom step, enter the room before you. The room is empty, except in the centre is a maple ornament stand with an old-fashioned locked bird cage upon it. Inside the cage is a white dove. The dove is the ultimate symbol of freedom. Now consider the limited choices you have allowed yourself to have in the past. These limited choices have affected you and your health and well-being. Look in the cage, and you will see that the dove has restricted movement within the cage, only a small choice of seed, and little or no interaction from others. It's time to set the dove free, so take the key from your pocket and carefully turn it in the lock on the cage.

Open the door and step back, it had been a while since freedom was an option, s/he may be timid at first, unsure of whether to take the options available to him/her. But you see now, <u>there are always choices, the freedom is there</u>, new and unknown, perhaps it is safer to remain a caged bird, to stick with what you know - but you've so longed for this freedom, to fly and move and be agile to sample the sweet, fresh delicious fruits of the world. You can choose now to stay always as you were, or to <u>take flight</u>. <u>Spread your wings and feel the will growing inside you</u>. Leave the caged past behind you choose freedom and fly. Be gone from this place, be free.

Memory Recall

Professional- This script is useful to help a client retrieve a lost memory or to help them remember where they have put something that has been misplaced. This process uses Ideomotor responses which should be explained to the client prior to beginning the trance, so the client can be aware that they are not expected to consciously move their fingers and to let the unconscious take control of their body and reactions.

It's good to know that <u>you can remember thoughts that were once forgotten.</u> Sometimes <u>just a little thing can trigger a memory</u>, a song that reminds you of a holiday or the smell of a perfume or aftershave that reminds you of someone you know. <u>You're remembering different things all of the time</u> and the truth is that <u>it is very simple thing to do, an easy thing to have happen and always when you're not expecting it.</u> These fleeting memories arrive at the moments when you're <u>most relaxed</u> and least expect them. A flicker of colour and suddenly <u>there it is, the one thing you've been looking for</u>. It's easy to remember, and so much easier when <u>you relax and let the memories come back to you</u> and then you don't even have to try to remember them, because <u>your mind is open to them already and you can just let them drift gently back to you</u> and can then communicate them to me, direct from your subconscious mind.

Your conscious mind can just <u>relax and sleep</u>. <u>Switch off,</u> because when you do, <u>your subconscious mind will open</u> and <u>all of the answers you seek will be there</u>, like opening a treasure chest and discovering the sparkling jewels that have been hidden inside. <u>You're unconscious</u> mind is responsible for taking care of you in many ways. It can repress memories for example, if it believes that doing so is the best thing for you. And I know that the one thing you would most like to <u>remember now</u> is *(state what it is the client wishes to remember)*. However your subconscious mind is very particular and very specific about following instructions.

So perhaps that conscious part of you can begin to integrate a new level of understanding and respect for your subconscious mind, to respect and understand that it works to protect you.

Now if there is presently any part of your consciousness still aware, switch it off, I want to talk directly to your subconscious which may not or will choose to provide you with a conscious memory of what you wish to remember.

Wait 3 minutes

If you are happy to communicate to me by speaking, then you can tell me now, by speaking, without disrupting the relaxation where *(state what it is the client wishes to remember)* is.

I'm going to pause for 10 seconds, for 5 seconds you can consider whether this is the right way to communicate *(state what it is the client wishes to remember)* For the subsequent 5 seconds you can give me the answer, if you will choose to do so. Consider this now. (Pause 10 sec)

If client does not give you the answer, continue with the following:

Thank you, I understand that you would like to communicate with me in another way. On your left hand I want you to use your fingers as a way of communicating to me.

Your pointing finger will be a "yes" finger, to communicate the answer "yes". Your middle finger on your left hand will be your "no" finger, to communicate the answer "no".

You can communicate your yes or no answers by moving the appropriate finger, by lifting it very clearly and keeping in a relaxed state. I will write down the responses you give me, which I can share at the end of the session. I will clarify with you at the end of my questioning whether you are happy for me to share the information you have given me, with him/her consciously. I want only for the questioning to be between myself and the subconscious. This means that *(client's name)* does not need to make any conscious effort to move his/her fingers, the subconscious can take control of the body now.

Ask closed questions and make notes on responses.

Time for Self

Amateur- Pre-frame to your client that now it is their time to relax. If any other thoughts invade this time, then instruct the client to replace these thoughts with relaxing memories. For example, having a relaxing bath. Also tell your client that they need to look after themselves, look after number one. Pre-frame that other people are doing the same for themselves. That they must take responsibility for their own health and well-being before others as only then can be in a fit state to help others.

This is your time now. Your time only, and although I can't say that all of the material issues will be solved at the end of this session, you will take with you a sense of peace and calm to enable you to let go and detach from the issues and stresses that used to cause you discomfort and even ill-health.

Let yourself drift deeper down now with each number I count and follow the prompts to enable you to relax 5 deeper down, sliding or floating passing stress and disappointment, 4 leaving aches and pains behind as you drift deeper down 3 choosing to ignore the attention demanded from others as you sink down now, letting go, 2 deeper and deeper down now, inside yourself where there is only your own desire for rest and peace and comfort. 1 releasing any fears or anxieties until there is only your own deep inner self. 0 now very deep, not trying, just letting go, there is only your deep inner self, unconcerned free spirited.

And I wonder where your vivid and intelligent creative imagination will allow you to drift now, where you have been most relaxed, with plenty of time, no demands now.

This is your time to relax comfortably, completely. If others should even dare to invade this space and time, you can tell them to go away. Tell them with the assertiveness that you usually restrain out of politeness, and when they have gone and you release that tension quickly recall relaxing times and memories. Perhaps relaxing in the sun, or even being at home, comfortably alone knowing that you have this time and space for yourself just to bathe your feet, (or paint your nails) or watch TV in your lounge.

Wherever you choose to be, <u>do something nice for yourself</u>. From now on, give yourself space and time. <u>Let go of any guilt or concerns for others</u>. Look after yourself completely and these are the reasons why you will begin to find yourself doing this more and more now and long after this session has ended.

Firstly, only you can take responsibility for your own health and well-being. To <u>achieve a good state of health and well-being</u> you need to give yourself space and time. Space and time and love for yourself to be calm and relax.

Only when you have achieved a positive and calm relaxed state of mind are you able to give your best to others. There is simply no point, therefore, in worrying about why others are stressing or doing until <u>you put yourself in a calm and relaxed state</u> to deal with them. <u>Do your best for yourself</u>, then you can do your best for others. But I don't want you to think about them very much. This is your holiday, your time away from them.

Look after yourself. Number one. Relax and go deeper 100 times deeper, 100 times better, 100 times more relaxed and happy.

And when you know that everyone around you is taking care of themselves, putting themselves first it will be even easier for you to <u>give time for yourself</u>, filling you with a growing sense of peace and tranquillity so that you are able to let go of all the things that you can't control and you really don't want to bother worrying about. As and when you do decide to share your time and space with others you will be in a much better state of mind to do it. <u>Feeling better and lighter and calmer and happier.</u>

Self Worth in Career.

Amateur - This script is useful for generating feelings of self worth, particularly when a client feels that they have not achieved all they have wanted to in their career.

As you continue to <u>rest and drift peacefully</u> into that comfortable place, I want you to become acutely aware that this time, here, now, is devoted entirely to you. It is your time, un-invaded for you to <u>heal and grow and change.</u> And although you may not consciously remember all of what I say, you are listening, and there will be changes, all of which are for your benefit and well-being.

And I want to talk to you now about self-worth - the value upon which you place your own abilities - all that you have ever been, all of what you are, and all of what you ever will be. I have listened to you talking now and can already tell you, that <u>you are much more valuable than you realise.</u> You have achieved more than you acknowledge and you are admired by others, even if you do not award this feeling to yourself.

Life is full of challenges, some big, some small. Sometimes it's a challenge to fit everything there is to do in one day, going to work, (feeding the kids), seeing family, exercising, learning more - it's a wonder you ever get time to yourself. And what would you do if you had that time? I'm sure you'd soon find something to keep yourself busy and so the quiet time also becomes a busy time. Busy, busy non-stop. <u>Except for now, you have stopped,</u> you have got time to look at your life and yourself and the value of what you have and who you have become. And there is a lot to value. There are so many people in the world who have nothing, who have achieved nothing who have nothing to take and nothing to give, some through no fault of their own. And it leaves them feeling so empty inside. And I know that at times before now, you may have sensed that emptiness around the edges, but let us put a better perspective on this, these feelings for you are unjust, unnecessary, for when you look at all you have - a good job, people who love you, a home, a wonderful powerful creative mind, a self healing body - capable of creating other unique and wonderful human beings.

And I know that these things did not occur to you by chance.

Yes the mind and the body were a gift, the abilities to think and communicate were taught to you, by those who loved you, but the other things, shall we say the material things, they were earned by you, <u>you can value</u> yourself for that without question.

I suspect that even if you do not know exactly when these feelings of low self esteem first started, that you are able to remember being a child and a time when you didn't even know what self esteem was, if you can remember how you looked or felt as a child, then I'd like you to <u>focus on that now</u>, perhaps you could see or hear that child playing. And as you watch him/her, you can see the people s/he loves and cares for interacting with him/her, encouraging him/her. Perhaps it is the first time s/he has tried something on his/her own, or learned something new, and you are aware of those around him/her, fussing over him/her, congratulating him/her. And you will see that as the years tick by, a pattern emerges, s/he does something well and gets praised, and throughout that time s/he soaks up all of this information and it lets him/her feel good about him/herself.

Now move forward in time and as s/he grows and moves on with him/her life, you will see that those whom s/he used to be so (praised) by are letting him/her grow, they are letting him/her spread his/her wings and fly the nest, no longer cocooned by them, <u>now independent and free.</u> With an everlasting bond of love between them. His/her own responsibility to nurture him/herself now. And s/he has coped well with this, but you will notice that s/he is much harder on his/herself than those who love him/her used to be. S/he drives him/herself much harder and praises his/herself much less than those who love him/her do.

And s/he did this to him/herself because s/he wanted the best of his/herself not to hurt or damage him/herself, and through drive and determination to create a good life for his/herself and his/her family and his/her future. S/he was becoming so successful - on a roll - at first and s/he kept pushing his/her boundaries beyond where s/he thought her limitations lay and surprising his/herself at all she could do. And s/he thought that this was all s/he needed. But you and I know that with all of the positive intention in the world, that is not enough. Perhaps the answer is not that s/he didn't love and value his/herself, but that s/he was so busy doing so well that s/he simply didn't have the time.

So now it is that time - time to go back in time, to any time that your subconscious now presents to you as appropriate, to go back and look at what you achieved at that time or how you coped and to say to yourself "well done", or be excited and jump around with yourself, or give yourself love or that passed self a hug. Give yourself a gift, a beautiful gift. This has been hard work, but you did it. Go to as many situations as you can find and make that other self, that past self, feel good about his/herself at all significant times and help him/her to acknowledge the value of his/herself. You may even be able to advise him/her of who s/he should be around to make his/herself feel good, as some people can help create those good feelings in the positive things they say to us. Be a mother to yourself, care for your delicate and complex feelings in the way you would nurture a child. Vow to praise yourself more in the future, to love and care for, your wonderful true self.

Your emotions are levelling, evening out, no longer the roller-coaster. Loving more, laughing more. More relaxed and happy and pleased with yourself, at peace with yourself, interrupting that self-critical voice to replace it with a more motherly one. Feelings of strength and comfort growing under complete control.

Self Image and Attractiveness

Professional- This script contains an anchoring process, which should be fully explained to the client before you begin any trance work. Ask the client to squeeze their fingers together when they feel good feelings during the trance.

As you <u>rest and relax more deeply</u> there than you have ever experienced before, <u>your mind is open to my suggestions</u> creating positive permanent changes which are all for your benefit and well being.

You know that you are a good kind person with many special qualities, that your true self is a fun and lively individual, happy and contented and respected. However, recently your fine and loving qualities have become hidden in a fog of uncertainty, your spirits dampened, you have become hidden in the fog unable to see yourself for who you really are and others unable to see the beauty beyond the fog, the beauty that is you and all that you have to offer.

As an intelligent bright individual, I know that you are immensely aware that attractiveness and self love are created using states of mind, not expensive items such as hair and makeup products/ expensive suits and cars for is it not true that those who think of themselves as ugly, and who focus on how ugly they feel, will always unconsciously sabotage any efforts to make themselves look and feel better.

I'm sure you've heard people say "look good, feel good". In the same way if you feel good, you're in a better frame of mind to make yourself look good, and so the two states, looking good and feeling good are constantly fuelling each other. The better you look, the better you feel and the better you look. And when you feel better, as you will, <u>you are actually becoming more attractive</u>. Think about people you consider to be attractive - friends or celebrities you have seen on the television. They enhance their attractiveness with their posture, physiology, their smile and the easy and confident way they communicate, and as a result they feel good about themselves and so they look healthy with clear skin, and a bigger smile.

The better they feel, the better they look and the cycle continues to create an image which others consider to be attractive. In fact you know, just from reflecting on the people you encounter that <u>everybody seems more attractive, just from a smile.</u> And the other fascinating thing that can happen is that the more <u>you belief in yourself, the more confident you</u> become and the more <u>others believe in you.</u> So if you, <u>believe yourself to be attractive and confident,</u> you project yourself to others as a confident, attractive person, and the more <u>you notice that others pay you compliments or congratulate you,</u> and you thank them and trust their honest compliments, the more and more <u>you believe in yourself as an attractive, confident person.</u>

So all of these wonderful, self-fulfilling cycles are created, and <u>every day in every way, you feel better and better.</u> I want you now to see, sense or imagine someone who you know to be attractive and confident. Notice what makes them <u>appear attractive</u> - is it their expression or an aura of calm and certainty, is it the way they stand? Or perhaps their assertiveness makes them attractive, there will of course be a certain amount of emphasis on that person's features, but remember that feel good - look good cycle and remember that attractiveness and self love are created via states of mind, not by hairstyles or expensive cars. Remember that attractiveness is not a physical quality but a state of mind which means that every intelligent person has the capabilities of achieving it as long as they know how to use their imagination.

Now I know that <u>you know how to use your imagination</u> because that is the wonderful state that hypnosis really is, and I can see that you have already achieved that state and that you are enjoying it. Now what you may not already know is that anything you practice during hypnosis uses the same parts of your brain that you will use when you are actually performing the behaviour or feelings when you wake up later. This for you means that during this time it is vital that you let yourself feel really good. <u>Feel fantastic to the best of your ability,</u> become a master of your own happiness so that you can allow those feelings to become a natural integral part of you when you wake later. So now, see sense or imagine yourself in the presence of that person you consider to be attractive and confident. You have noted their physiology and state of mind that you consider to be attractive. Now, step into that person's body so that you become that attractive person - notice how you instantly feel better, look down at what you are wearing and love how attractive that makes you feel. Try walking and enjoy the posture, the stride, the head held high, eyes wide and bright, notice your breathing now and where in your body those good feelings are coming from, which direction those good feelings are moving in and if that feeling of confidence and attractiveness had a colour, what colour would it be? Now stand tall, bathe yourself in that special colour and smile in this attractive body. Love yourself, let yourself feel really good then squeeze together your thumb and your finger. Feel that you know all of the secrets to looking and feeling this way.

Now that you have anchored in yourself all of the wonderful feelings of feeling attractive and confident, you will be able to access those feelings for a "top-up" at any time after you awake, simply by squeezing together your thumb and finger.

Now slowly drift out of that body, thank the person for teaching you these new, wonderful skills and feelings, and relax and drift deeper. In a few moments, I'm going to reach over and lift your hand, then I am going to give you some further suggestions and as I do so, you will find that your hands starts to drift quite naturally and automatically down without your conscious awareness of it doing so. When your hand touches your lap, this will serve as an indication of agreement that the necessary changes have occurred in your subconscious and that your feelings and behaviour will dramatically improve for the betterment of your self-image, confidence, happiness and attractiveness.

(Raise the client's hand)

Now continue to relax and go deeper for you will find, day by day, no matter what you are doing you <u>relax and feel better</u>. If you are doing something you relax and enjoy it more, you enjoy yourself more, comfortably, you <u>feel more confident about yourself and what you are doing</u> and saying so you become much more in control of how you feel. <u>You feel in control and build your self confidence</u>, your self-acceptance, your self-esteem; you squeeze your fingers and feel fantastic. These suggestions are in your unconscious mind permanently as you <u>drift deeper down.</u>

You will even find that as you feel better about yourself, that you will be able to tolerate the persons, places or things that used to aggravate you and annoy you. You will be able to <u>adjust yourself to situations</u> even when you cannot change them as nothing stops you feeling good, nothing removes your certainty.

And as this happens you will find yourself better able to achieve for yourself that picture of yourself that you have in your mind, of how you want to be, as you can be, as you will be. You will be able to <u>stand up for yourself</u>, and state your opinion or suggestion without awkwardness, without fear, without anxiety, much stronger, <u>the person you have become</u>. The things that used to bother you - you no longer give so much attention - that attention you now give to yourself and feeling really good.

Confidence

Amateur - this script helps the client to get in touch with previous feeling of confidence to use them now and in the future.

Now relax <u>more deeply than before</u>, so relaxed and at ease. Telling yourself "I can, I will, I have my very own best interests at heart."

You see you have told me that your confidence has been an issue for you in the past. Yet the person with little confidence did not email/call me did not take steps to sort the problem out. The person without confidence would not call at all, and did not have an appointment to show up. For It took a certain confidence to get yourself here today.

I will speak to you now, you can make those changes that you really wish to make, for <u>you're unconscious</u> mind is listening and will receive and act upon the messages it hears. And you will find, as this is happening, that you become much happier, within yourself. So much more…delighted with who you are, what you have and everything you can offer.

Can you remember a time where you have felt feelings of confidence, perhaps in a different situation to the experiences you have had recently? And you can, remember how you stood, and walked and talked, clearly, remember now at the time, <u>it's very easy to behave in this way.</u>

Thinking about what you really do want to achieve here, your outcome to be relaxed and at ease now with who you are and all of your amazing and special qualities not to be denied, for you know, it matters not who is judging you, what they might be thinking, you can never really know that and so it doesn't matter anyway.

What matters is what you are thinking and focusing on. All of your unique and special qualities - remember them? Those abilities to <u>relax and be at ease</u> feeling cool and calm, as somebody asks you, your jaw relaxed, like an elastic band letting go, allowing you to think and communicate your true thoughts clearly, coolly. Just breathing, in and out, unconsciously, all the time.

You can enjoy and look forward to being a mother/father to yourself because you know that, you can't know the situations or conversations that the inner child may have, but you will always be there, offering good positive advice.

Coaching, caring and encouraging the correct sort of behaviour. Defusing panic. Telling yourself you'll be fine, you can achieve this easily, you have so much more potential and I will help you access it. You can let go of the things that might be or might not be but will probably never be as bad as you used to imagine them to be, because you trust yourself now to get on with it, when the time comes.

That's the only way to do it. Since you find now, that <u>your mind is so filled with happy, positive calming thoughts,</u> you don't really have time to analyse or construct or destruct over things that might not even happen anyway.

You know that if and when the time comes, you will be saying positive things to yourself, looking for the best possible outcome and looking as if you really mean business. <u>You can do this easily, can't you?</u>

Because even if your confidence has been hidden away, only to be found in old memories, or even only to be seen in others, it is there, you have it, otherwise you wouldn't even know what it was or how to use it, but you do, don't you?

Improve confidence

Professional - This script utilises a technique with the clients "timeline." Therefore you must establish the direction of the timeline, prior to induction & deepener as some timelines will go front to back, and others may go left to right. You may want to adjust this script to suit the timeline of your client.

Now I want you to just imagine how you look now, sat there in that chair, relaxing, <u>breathing deeply</u>. Imagine how relaxed and comfortable your body would look, if you were able to <u>rise out of it and see yourself there.</u> You know that when you are sleeping, a special hormone chemical is released in your body to keep it settled and still so that you do not physically act out your dreams. Imagine how you would look there in that chair, comfortably still.

Now rise above your body, and imagine you are able to <u>look down</u> upon yourself from the ceiling, from the roof, from the sky and <u>up and up and back and back</u> until you are looking down on yourself as small as a grain of sand, back and back into a new dimension, where as you look down upon where you were you see your time-line. Your life past, you; where you are now, and your future ahead of you. Now float towards the line that symbolises your life and hover above it where you can get a clear view of each significant event - past, present and future.

Now float over your past and go back to when you were very young, probably before the age of seven, when someone or something happened to cause you to suffer some damage to your level of confidence. It doesn't matter if this event was not truly the first time, nor if it seems insignificant now, nor if it is even part or all fantasy, what matters is that we utilise the information presented by your subconscious mind.

So look down on that event from up here and just have an idea of what is happening in this scene.

Now I want you to move along your line of life to 15 minutes after the event has happened, and notice what you are doing in that scene. From your position above your line of life, I want you to send love and confidence and any other resources to that younger you that you needed at that time to make that younger you feel comforted 15 minutes after the event happened. Now float back to the time of the event happening. And from the safety of your line of life, look down at the time of the event happening and send down to that younger you the resources you needed at that particular time.

Whether it was the ability to speak up or to know how to protect yourself, so that whatever was said or done would not affect your self worth. Send the resources now to you at the time of experiencing the event.

Now when you have done that, I want you to travel back across your line of life to 15 minutes before the event happened, or back to a time where there were no bad feelings because the event had not yet happened. And as you look down on that time I want you to send down to yourself and to all others involved all of the resources required that would have made this situation different, and less troublesome. Perhaps you would send to yourself a great deal of self-confidence. And perhaps you would send some maturity or stability to the other people involved.

Perhaps as you see the event from this new perspective, you can see others fear, hurt and damage. Perhaps you can <u>send some healing love</u> to all involved now.

Now with all of your resources inside of you, float along your line of life back to the time of the event happening. With all of your resources cocooning and protecting you go down toward your line of life into the time of the event, into your own body at that time, seeing it through your own younger eyes. As you see it now, notice how <u>you're feeling differently, stronger, detached</u>. Protected now, this event no longer bothersome. When you are sure that all of your work is done, float out of that event and up and above your line of life - forward and look down onto the present day again. See yourself sat there in the chair and send down to yourself powers of self confidence, self worth and assertiveness.

Now look forward along your line of life and float above an event one week from now. <u>See yourself being confident and assertive at work, speaking clearly and with certainty</u>. See yourself <u>at home, at work, socialising with confidence and certainty</u>.

Look forward along your line of life to one month from now and <u>see yourself at home, at work, socialising with confidence and certainty.</u>

Look forward along your line of life to one year from now and <u>see yourself at home, at work, socialising with confidence and certainty.</u>

Now rise up and above your line of life so that all of it is within your view. See all of the past situations where your confidence wavered in the past have changed. And see in all of your future events, yourself acting and reacting confidently and projecting yourself with certainty right up until the end of your days.

Move along your line of life and float above the moment of now. Then drift with confidence and certainty. Down and down through space and time, through the sky, lower than the ceiling and back into your body and then open your eyes.

Confidence within a Team

Amateur - Use this script for those who want to develop their confidence to allow them to speak up and join in more when in a group environment.

I know in the past you have felt frustration at that inability to speak up in group situations. And this is not due to your motivation to do it. <u>You know that you want to do it</u> and that <u>it is of value to many aspects of your confidence,</u> and <u>the positive impact it could have on your career and opportunities</u> in the future. You are extremely motivated to move away from this problem and towards your future of confidence where you will find yourself comfortable in sharing your valuable thoughts and ideas, the equal of all others, <u>relaxed and comfortable</u>. For when you have something to say, you say it.

Firstly you will study the other team members and how it is that they communicate and add to the group. You need not do anything more than that, simply watch and listen. You might notice the pitch or volume with which a team member offers his/her comments, and how others pay attention and respond to this, so as to keep themselves within the loop and offer interest to what is being said.

Perhaps the person about to offer a comment, leans forward before speaking or takes a breath in or moves their hand in a gesturing way. <u>You can notice the non-verbal communication that each person makes before speaking,</u> so as to attract attention to what they are about to say. You could notice who they look at, or where their eyes are as they speak. They may make eye contact with each person or just with one person or they may be looking up into their head to find the right language to communicate their thoughts. And as <u>you note these things in the comfort of your</u>

mind, just relax and notice how others respond to the person communicating to the group. For they are all members of the team and even if they are not verbalising their communication, they are acknowledging the comments of the speaker - that is what makes it a team. So what are these people doing in response to the speaker, watching, frowning, smiling, nodding, looking up into their own heads for their own thoughts, their own responses? They haven't even spoken and you could probably make an accurate guess about what they are thinking because you are a master of communication. You have been practicing it for years!

You will see that these people seem to communicate so naturally, so automatically and the reason why is because it is not an unusual thing to do, it is not odd or bizarre behaviour. The comments are made as easily as breathing. When you practice, it just flows.

The great thing about hypnosis, relaxing in this way is that you are able to practice anything you want to do or be. And the amazing and fascinating thing is that as you do so, your brain works and creates the same neural pathways, as if you are actually doing it. This means that when you do actually do it, the behaviour is comfortable and familiar, natural and automatic, as easy as breathing. So that the next time you are here, comfortable and relaxed in this way, having studied the group communication patterns of your colleagues, or you can do it now if you remember and visualise them, you can imagine that you are participating in that team conversation and try out all of these gestures and tones and volumes that you have witnessed others using. Try them out to see which one would work for you, what you are comfortable with. Perhaps you will be nodding to acknowledge somebody else's comments before taking a breath and leaning in, your voice clear, speaking only slightly louder than normal, using whatever style you choose. Even if you do not actually speak, you will use much more non-verbal communication than before, so that others realise you are an active listening, communicating member of the team. When <u>you will speak,</u> you can decide if you will be looking at one particular person, or seeking acknowledgement from all of the team by offering them each some eye contact.

To begin with, <u>you may find yourself more at ease</u> to practice responding to an individual within the group and pretending that all of the others are blurred into the background at that time of your speaking, as if you are having an ordinary one to one chat. <u>Keep doing this in your mind</u>. You know that in the past you have held in comments, that are made and acknowledged by others. <u>Let your thoughts and ideas be free, let them flow.</u>

We live in a land of equal opportunities, democracy and freedom of speech. Give yourself the opportunity that you would offer to any other like you, who came to you for guidance and support. <u>Relax</u> the harsh filters of your precious thoughts <u>and ease</u> some of that over-controlling self-doubt. Utilise your conversational skills in a way that can allow you to <u>be proud of who you are and all that you have to offer</u>, to develop the feeling of <u>feeling really good about yourself</u>, and to give the opportunity for others to see more potential, more intelligence and more skill within you.

IPS (Inter Personal Skills)

Amateur - Use this script for clients who want to improve their communication skills in a subtle way, such as by focusing on their body language and tone of voice.

More and more every day you will become aware of how every part of you makes and receives communication with others. And what you will start to notice is that way in which people with very good rapport with each other, talk in the same kind of language, they enjoy similar things and their body move with a likeness. Most people, who do this, do it unconsciously, however, great communicators also emulate this behaviour in order to gain better rapport with the person they are communicating with - and <u>this is</u>

something you can do too, to help improve your interpersonal skills. It is called matching and mirroring.

You can match people in conversation - using the same types of words in your language as they like to use - you might even notice if they have a particular sensory preference, you might notice them saying "I see it like this" which tells you that the person is very visual, or "it sounds to me like this" which tells you that the person prefers to use their auditory skills and language; or perhaps they "feel this way" which tells you that the person is very kinaesthetic and uses emotional and tactile language more. If you feed back to that person in their own sensory preference they will feel much more at ease with you because they will think that you are similar to them, and we all get on better with people and feel more comfortable, with people much more like ourselves.

Two ears and one mouth- listen to people twice as much as you talk, it's the only way to learn.

Now relax and go deeper, for you know with absolute certainty that this new skill, that you can be aware of developing, will become much more natural and automatic every day, in every way.

And you can match people's tone of voice, speed of talking and mirror their body language and gestures - not so as they'd notice, not at exactly the same time, but gracefully and when appropriate. When you know, and you will know when, that person feels at ease with you, then you can begin to change your body language, tone and communication to get across your thoughts and feelings, and because you have built such good rapport with that person, you'll find that you begin to impact upon that person and that they, quite unconsciously begin to match and mirror you and that is the control that you have - you can actually begin to change that persons thoughts and feelings!

Now relax and go deeper, for you know with absolute certainty that this new skill, that you can be aware of gently developing, will become much more natural and automatic every day in every way.

And when you find yourself stuck with a person whom you want to break rapport with, you simply do the opposite of everything I tell you, but since you want to make new friends, you won't do this very often anyway.

More and more every day, you will become aware of how much <u>more relaxed and happy you seem to be in conversational situations</u>. And the more <u>you relax, the more easily information for you to share will come to you</u> and <u>the better you feel and the more you relax.</u> Confidence encourages confidence so the more you have in your abilities the more others will have in you and <u>this will make you feel good and confident within yourself.</u>

Conversation flows from and to you as naturally as breathing and <u>as you relax,</u> you draw upon your vast knowledge and information to share with others, comfortable asking questions and modestly sharing your own experiences.

Any brief periods of silence can be used to reflect upon the conversation you have already had, to praise yourself on how <u>easily and freely you are talking</u> and to allow any other thoughts that you would share to emerge clearly into your mind. If you ever feel awkward during a period of silence or, more likely sense that the other person feels awkward during a period of silence, you could even express how you used to feel a little uncomfortable and ill at ease in these sorts of situations in the past and how you've managed to change that.

<u>Now relax and go deeper, much, much deeper down,</u> for you know with absolute certainty that these new skills, that you can be gently aware of developing, will become much more natural every day.

And you appreciate much more, your magnetic personality that you utilise to its fullest potential. Comfortable in paying and receiving compliments as you take a few moments now to <u>see your future self, happy and relaxed and receiving an abundance</u>

of compliments, causing you to feel really good about yourself and so confident, relaxed and happy.

Take a few moments to indulge in this future and when you know that you have received agreement from your subconscious mind that it will follow each of the instructions I have given you today in exactly the way I have said; then you will feel yourself beginning to wake and when your subconscious mind has made these changes your eyes will open and you will be wide awake and feeling wonderful. So take your time and do this now and I will see you in a few moments when you open your eyes.

Positive Inner Voice.

Amateur - This script is very useful for clients who use negative self-talk and put themselves down a lot. It encourages them to be kinder to themselves which will in turn help them to feel better about themselves.

We all have that inner voice, that part of ourselves inside of ourselves that responds to our thoughts and actions. But what everyone doesn't know is the impact that that inner voice has on the way we feel, which in turn affects the way we behave. And what even less people know is that you are in control of that inner voice you can control the language it uses, the tone of the voice it has - you can do these things so that it makes you feel good or better about yourself which will in turn, affect the way you behave.

All you need to do is learn how to change it, alter it and interrupt it. And you're going to learn how to do this now, and when you have learned it you will use it and when you use it you will soon realise that you can experience some wonderful now feelings and reactions and wonderful feedback to the way you now react differently.

So here's what you do. You find yourself in a situation that would normally have made you uncomfortable and you hush your thoughts for a moment to enable yourself to hear what your inner voice is telling you and what emotions are whizzing around your system and, you quite literally <u>take control.</u> You say to yourself "stop." In a firm - but not aggressive way. You <u>take a deep breath and expel with your outward breath any tension.</u> Straighten yourself up, widen your eyes and ask yourself what is it that I need to say or do - and run through it in your mind <u>imagining the precise way you want to say or do it</u> - And imagining it going well will make you feel so much <u>calmer and happier,</u> then you tell yourself with that inner voice in you kindest words and most motivating tone "that's it - that's the ticket, now let's do it for real" and that inner voice coaches and persuades you to do the things that <u>you really want to do and to achieve the things that you are capable of achieving much more easily</u> than you had ever imagined.

That inner voice will encourage you, not bully you, into taking the first steps that you will make. And when you have made them, it will praise you like an internal celebration, shaking you by the hand, patting you on the back and congratulating you.

And you can know the power of that inner voice, for in the past you have allowed it to criticise, bully and express disappointment and oh, how that has held you back, these negative inner thoughts really didn't achieve that positive confident state and what I say to that is this "If what you're doing isn't working, do something different." And you'll find that <u>you'll enjoy much more,</u> listening to that encouraging motivating voice and <u>you'll enjoy the change</u> in the way that you feel and <u>you'll enjoy the change in your behaviour</u> and <u>you'll enjoy the increase in rewards that this brings.</u>

Now to be sure that you will get this right there is only one other thing that you need to do, and that is to change your physiology. Make yourself <u>look happy and confident and positive -</u> even when you do not feel those things, encourage yourself into the positive posture of a happy confident person - smile, lift your head, widen your eyes, open your body and then just try to feel those rotten old feelings and think those rotten old thoughts - you can't - it's physically impossible to try to create negative feelings when your body is in a happy confident posture.

~

Fears and Phobias

~

Dispersing Anxiety Sickness

Amateur - For some, anxiety can lead to feelings of nausea as well as the general tension and negative thinking. This script helps the anxious client to feel settled in their mind and their body.

Your body; <u>very good</u> - it tells you what you need to know - <u>relax, it says</u> I'm giving you this message, <u>just listen and follow my instructions</u>, you're going to find more time; <u>this time is for you now.</u>

<u>You can do that easily</u> because you want the bad feelings to recede, reduce and disappear. Every day in every way feeling better and better. Through the night, any memories that need to be dealt with can be done in your dreams where you can say the words that needed to be said, and later, when you wake, the dreams will be over and those problems will have escaped in your sleep. You will be refreshed, relaxed and curious about your day.

<u>There is so much to wonder about.</u> The future, never predictable, you can never know what to expect when you awake each morning for every day is new and fresh. One day in the past, a long while ago, you woke and felt unsettled, anxious about something that was going to occur later that day. That is gone, it has happened and it is gone, it is in the past. And now as you sleep a gentle mist falls, softly and calmly, <u>down and down</u> counteracting the acidity in the earth, dissolving and settling until in the morning the world will wake, refreshed, relaxed and anxious about how things will be new and different every day.

And when later you wake, each morning new and fresh wondering all of the wonderful things you can create in your day and <u>all that there is to look forward to,</u> the critical thoughts and feelings gone. <u>You are on a journey of discovery</u>, enquiring about the new and wonderful way in which you can <u>achieve a deep connection with yourself, in a way that settles you</u> like a calming dissolving mist, <u>drifting down</u> around you. And throughout the day, if anyone is making increasing demands upon you or even you upon yourself, you say to them what needs to be said, and ensure that what you need them to do, or not to do, is done or not done.

You internally dissolve negative emotions, and bring to your awareness, only happy feelings. Happy, positive and healthy feelings are now easy to bring into your awareness, you gently access them and the calm and warmth that comes with them dissolves the negative emotions until they evaporate completely.

You find yourself, paying attention to yourself using the most natural ways to re-hydrate your body. Washing away the toxins and chemicals that in the past were over created, you do not need them, functioning now in a balanced, easy going and tranquil way inside and outside of you. You see and feel only good things happening to you.

Tapping into the simplest things that make all the difference, the calming seas after the storm are now just gentle waves, lapping on a cool, smooth shore. Can you imagine this? Can you actually feel this restful scene occurring in your mind. Wash away the impurities into the gentle sea where the vast oceans will dissolve it completely.

And later, when you wake feeling refreshed and relaxed and curious about your day, you'll be surprised to discover a feeling of calm gently cleansing continually washing over you. You might like to try to feel as bad as you used to and be curious to discover how things have changed. Every day is new so you can never know what to expect, never believe that you know what is coming tomorrow morning, you do not, and you can enjoy the uncertainty of discovering and the certainty of knowing that tomorrow will occur with ease. Just the way you want it.

Combat Fear of Flying (with Anchoring)

*Professional - Pre-frame with the client that you will create a resource anchor on their knuckle whilst they are in trance where the * is displayed. If you intend to create a light trance only, the client can create* *the anchor themselves using a finger squeeze.*

Now that you rest so comfortably there, <u>continuing to relax…</u> I'd like your mind to drift to a place of safety. Perhaps there perhaps here, you can notice how safe you are feeling there. It may be someone or something, perhaps something you can see, or an awareness of its presence by a secure feeling inside of you. It doesn't matter where you are or who you are with, all that matters is that it makes you feel <u>really good and very, very safe and secure.</u> Notice if there are any sounds or smell that allow the feelings of safety to envelop you.

Think of a colour… that represents this feeling of safety, make that colour more intense, brighter more vivid and as it grows in you and around you…with <u>the pleasant sounds of your safety overcoming any other thoughts or noises,</u> wherever you go. As the colour grows brighter, the comfort becomes immense, you'll be surprised that the many places in which you notice this colour now. (In a moment I will touch your knuckle, and when I do so, this will create a link between the touch and your feeling of safety. This means that whenever you or I touch your knuckle in the future, you will also automatically experience this feeling of safety.)

Now let's first be sure that this feeling of safety is at its peak. Feel now, <u>completely safe, happy, loved calm and secure.</u> Can <u>you remember those times</u>? Seeing those wonderful things, hearing what you heard and <u>feeling totally safe, happy, loved, calm and secure</u> make the colours bright, notice how the feelings inside of you move more assertively and that's right, indulging yourself in those sounds. *

<u>Experience that complete and total safety and security again and again,</u> perhaps using the same memory, perhaps a different one. Can you <u>notice how is it is to feel so good now?</u> Feel now completely safe, happy, loved calm and secure. Can <u>you remember those times?</u> Seeing those wonderful things, hearing

what you heard and feeling <u>totally safe, happy, loved, calm and secure</u> make the colours bright, <u>notice how the feelings inside of you move more assertively and that's right, indulging yourself in those sounds. *</u>

(Repeat again if necessary to stack the anchor.)

And now, with those feelings, locked inside of you, in your mind, we are going to go on a journey. Perhaps you can imagine a holiday, or remember a time in the past when you were travelling by plane. It's up to you... If you remember a time, I want you to notice how <u>you are *now* able to take this flight in a calm and confident manor, feeling totally safe</u>. If you choose to create a time in your mind, that is fine too. You are going to be using your imagination so <u>you are in control, and you will keep yourself totally safe.</u> Did you know that whenever you imagine something in your mind, you use all the same neural networks as if you were actually participating in the act? In this way, <u>you are practising being successful, you are practicing feeling good as you fly.</u>

So begin now, perhaps your journey begins at home, with your luggage ready by the door. Maybe you will drive to the airport, or perhaps a taxi will take you. Now think about where you will be in just a few hours time, the people who will be there, how the weather will be.

Double- checking that your feelings and everything is in order... <u>You have with you everything you need. You have tightly packed your feeling of safety inside of you</u>. As you make your way to the airport now, take a few moments to fully <u>glide into your feeling of safety.</u> Allow the secure feeling to grow from there, gently glowing and flowing with warmth and comfort, out to the tips of your fingers, up to the top of your head and down to the tips of your toes...and should you wish to...<u>you can remain in this relaxed state all the way there.</u>

When you arrive you busy yourself with the checking in process, looking for the right place to be. <u>You are aware of how</u>

calm and relaxed everyone around you seems to be, chatting and calm and whenever you want or need to, you recall those safe feelings. Fully involve yourself in your secure place, and as you are aware here, now, of everything in the outside world serving to aid your calm and relaxed feelings. This place... it simply doesn't bother you... it's just a place that you're passing through, but the relaxation remains like a familiar friend looking after you massaging you, offering you reassuring suggestions. You are even able to maintain this as you move through the queue and check in.

Allow the feelings to remain and soften as you move through the airport towards the departure lounge. Perhaps you can look around the airport shops and choose a book to read on the plane, something you can be completely engrossed in. Something that you would like to sit down and read right now...so you fly it (*Hypnotherapist say the sentence as "so you fly it" instead of "so you buy it"*) and settle down, beginning to read... with your feeling of safety gently dancing in the corner of your mind, ready to be activated whenever you need it.

Time will pass as you wait for your flight-time passing sometimes slowly and sometimes quickly and you remain fully occupied and at ease as you wait.

Every now and then when you think of the flight to come and go, you may experience a feeling of "butterflies" inside which you recognise as gentle excitement and anticipation. To calm yourself you apply your anchor * just like so. That's it, again allowing yourself to be involved with that safe familiar feeling, comfortable, warm and relaxed place, shinning from you inside outwards, taking complete care of you, ensuring you are loved, cared for blessed and safe. *

Keep the feeling fully tuned in and turned up as you queue for your flight, helping the feeling to continue steadily with each easy breath you take. Each outward breath relaxing your muscles and breathing out any tension at all.

As you board the aircraft, involve yourself in the complete

feeling of safety. Imagine it is a bubble of safety surrounding you and your family, keeping you safe and secure. Your bubble remains around you, the safest place possible as you take your seat, ready to rise up to meet your goals.

You may not now be able to see the details of everyone and everything around you. Know that the safe feelings you experience now are real and will remain with you in this situation in the future. The feelings you have now are the ones that confirm you are absolutely safe * as the plane begins to move across the runway, gathering swiftness and gently lifts off the ground.

Know now that by returning to your place of safety, you can glide the journey with ease, in control, with complete confidence.

Again allow the safe feelings to soften, so that you can become absorbed in your book, have a conversation or order a drink. If at any time you feel those gentle excited butterflies inside you beginning to flutter, know that you can return to your relaxed and safe state at any time. *

Sooner than you think the plane begins to slowly and steadily descend. You take a moment to evaluate your journey and praise yourself for your calm and relaxed attitude throughout. With a sense of pride and with ease and grace you return to your normal state on the earth with much more confidence in preparation for your next journey. What will you say to your friends and family to describe your wonderful experience?

Metaphor for Ignoring Phobias

Amateur - This metaphor helps the client to distract their attention from the thing that they become phobic about. Use this script in conjunction with the NLP Fast Phobia Cure or with another phobia script. Use this script on its own for mild fears only.

There once was a keen gardener who tended to a beautiful rose garden not too far from here. He grew the most beautiful romantic roses you could ever imagine. Every colour of the rainbow, strong with petals as soft as luxury velvet and a strong, sweet perfumed aroma that would overwhelm you as you walked past the garden. The roses were precious, like memories, they had been planted for significant times or events, each one had a different story, some happy, some sad, some for those he had loved, some for those he had lost. And he came to the garden, every day to take care of these memories which gave him a sense of peace and love, as well as being the one place in the world where he could <u>come to relax and escape</u> from the challenging and demanding world.

One day, the diligent gardener was trimming the dead flower from one of his most beautifully coloured rose bushes, <u>you know the colour I mean</u>, and as he did so, a thorn broke from the plant and entered his thumb, the man swore and cursed and although the wound was bleeding he was unable to remove the thorn from inside his thumb. He went home that night and bathed his thumb in warm water and bicarbonate of soda, but still the thorn would not budge.

Eventually his wife told him to leave it. She said "<u>your body is an intelligent organism. It will always expel the things it no longer requires and you do not need to worry about it doing that. Just relax and let it do its job. It has been doing this so many years that I'm sure it has a better idea about what to do than you do.</u>" So the gardener went to bed that night with the thorn from the rose still lodged in his thumb. In the morning when the gardener had awoke, for a few moments he had forgotten about his thumb, then, when he checked it, he found that the thorn was no longer there, his body had expelled it - and with good reason and it was resting, clean in the corner of his bed.

Well you would think that to be the end of the story but in fact it is not, the gardener went back to work that morning to continue tending to the gardens as normal. Except he found himself to be extremely cautious of the thorns, which for so long had not been a bother to him. He was so anxious in fact that not only was he seeing thorns all over the place, he began to count them and certain that he could no longer abide them he removed them all. He worked so frenziedly, he didn't notice the sun shining, or the beautiful smell of the flowers or the colours or even when the sky clouded and began to rain. That night he went home shattered and exhausted but certain that he had removed all the thorns from each plant.

When his wife looked at him she enquired as to what the matter was and when he told her she simply said "this obsession will not do your health any good." The next day (which I think was a Thursday), the gardener returned to work, horrified to discover that every rose bush and plant had begun to re-grow its thorns. At a loss, the gardener made a conscious decision to ignore the thorns. He said to himself "Don't look at the thorns, don't touch the thorns, I will not get cut or scratched by these thorns." Yet despite his thoughts and efforts the gardener became even more cut and scratched than he had ever been in all of his working life. As he sat down in despair looking down at his hands and how bad they appeared to look, a magician who had been watching the gardener for sometime came to offer some advice.

The gardener told the magician all about the thorns and how he just couldn't seem to get rid of the problem because the thorns kept on growing and how when he'd said to himself in his head "Don't look at the thorns, don't touch the thorns, I will not get cut or scratched by the thorns," that he had become more cut and scratched than ever before.

So the magician explained that in life you get more of what you focus on and the gardener said - "I wasn't focusing on the thorns, I was telling myself not to!" So the magician said, "Don't look at the thorns" presupposes that there are thorns and that you can see them and touch them. 'I will not get cut or scratched by the thorns presupposes that not only are there thorns, but they have the ability to cut and scratch you."

"So what is the solution? The solution is to focus on what you *do* want more of - <u>have you noticed the scent of the flowers today, or the new bud over there - just opening, or the cool breeze, or the sound of the children playing?</u>" The gardener had not noticed any of these things.

He said "No, I've been too busy thinking about -" And at that point the magician cast a spell. He didn't magic away all of the thorns, he didn't make them invisible either the problem was still there, a natural problem, <u>there for a good reason</u>. What the magician did was quite simply to make the gardener focus only on the most beautiful elements of the roses, the smells, the colours, and the feel of the velvety petals.

And what happened is the focus became the reality and <u>the problems that were no longer focused on, were no longer there.</u> So although the gardener couldn't make the thorns go away, he learned not to focus on them and focus instead on all of the good and wonderful things. <u>His beliefs became his reality so now there is no pain and only love and roses.</u>

Metaphor for Needle Phobia

Amateur - This is a lovely hypnotic script that uses lots of secret language. When you say particular words to a client in trance, they will not consciously hear the secret language, but unconsciously they will receive the messages you are giving them.

Long, long ago there lived a family community of people who relied on the magical waters of a secret spring, to feel better and to <u>move easily and be injected with goodness and vitality.</u> But the spring was hidden in the depths of a dragon's lair and each new century a townsperson was nominated as the collector of the magical waters.

This century the town folk had nominated a young man called John. Although he appeared quiet and reserved he was a deep thinker and the people had faith that he would be able to come up with an effective strategy to pass the dragon and receive the magical spring water so desperately needed to keep everyone well.

(Hypnotherapist say "Needles to say" instead of "Needless to say")
Needles to say, in the early days John was not happy about the prospect of facing a dragon, and having his skin pierced by its sharp teeth just to get to the magical waters that would heal his body. And after a time he began to really worry when he knew that the injection day was drawing nearer. But the town's folk continued to push him and encourage him <u>for his own good as well as their own.</u>

One day John decided not to go to collect the magical spring water, he decided that it really was an unpleasant experience being scratched and bitten by the dragon and he just couldn't do it anymore. The townsfolk were worried and tried to convince him but he refused and became upset and *they* became more and more frustrated and in the end they tied him to a wagon and drove him there themselves. Now you might be asking yourself why it is that someone else couldn't have gone and got the water but you see John had been nominated at the turn of the century and would have to continue until the next turn of the century so you can understand why <u>it is important John begins to feel more comfortable with the appointments.</u>

When the wagon arrived at the edge of the dragon's lair the townsfolk untied John and pushed him into the cave. He struggled and grappled with the dragon, finally succumbing to just a small scratch on his arm before the dragon lost interest and allowed him to collect the magical waters from the spring and pass quietly by the dragon back to his village.

For a while, whilst there remained magical water keeping the people well, <u>John didn't even think about the dragon</u>. But again the time came when he had only a few days to prepare to make the journey. John became anxious and worried but to his good fortune, a caring relative had sought the assistance of a wise sprite who would meet John half way on his journey to the dragon's lair. John was not feeling enthusiastic about any part of the journey, though keen to overcome his fears and to benefit from the healing powers available to him he set out on his journey.

Along the way John tried to put what lay ahead to the back of his mind but as his body became weaker and more tense it was difficult not to hope that the healing injection of spring water would make him feel so much more flexible, well and invigorated.

He took a moment to dwell on all of the things that his fellow villagers took for granted: Going to clubs, driving their wagons and playing sports and he suddenly had a real urge to overcome his fear of the dragon so that he could collect as much healing fluid as he required. With his mind focused to a needlepoint at that moment he stumbled across the sprite.

The sprite sat on a creaking log, reading a book of wisdom and humming in a gentle piercing tone. John sat down and the sprite looked up from her book. She said in her gentle piercing voice "I want you to imagine being inside of yourself and locate within yourself the parts of yourself that it would be helpful to change. You might need to gently persuade yourself, to make these changes effective, because you had created them for a positive reason, perhaps to protect yourself in some way.

But looking back; (Hypnotherapist say "on-injection" instead of "on reflection") on-injection, you can see that those old behaviours were not appropriate and so now persuade which ever parts need to be gently coerced into behaving much more smoothly and calmly in the future. I know that you try not to think about it and I wonder if you can just as easily choose to forget those old uncomfortable feelings, and your mind can choose only the most pleasant things to remember and everything else you can forget to think about.

Your memory is always forgetting oversights what it has got over and done with and you can forget all of the discomfort and confusion and remembering to be calm and relaxed merely

te who would meet John half way on his journey to the
gon's lair. John was not feeling enthusiastic about any part of
journey, though keen to overcome his fears and to benefit from
healing powers available to him he set out on his journey.

Along the way John tried to put what lay ahead to the back of
mind but as his body became weaker and more tense it was
icult not to hope that the healing injection of spring water
uld make him feel so much more flexible, well and invigorated.
He took a moment to dwell on all of the things that his fellow
agers took for granted: Going to clubs, driving their wagons
playing sports and he suddenly had a real urge to overcome
fear of the dragon so that he could collect as much healing
d as he required. With his mind focused to a needlepoint at
t moment he stumbled across the sprite.

The sprite sat on a creaking log, reading a book of wisdom and
nming in a gentle piercing tone. John sat down and the sprite
ked up from her book. She said in her gentle piercing voice "I
nt you to imagine being inside of yourself and locate within
urself the parts of yourself that it would be helpful to change.
might need to gently persuade yourself, to make these
nges effective, because you had created them for a positive
son, perhaps to protect yourself in some way.

But looking back; (Hypnotherapist say "on-injection" instead of
reflection") on-injection, you can see that those old behaviours
re not appropriate and so now persuade which ever parts need
be gently coerced into behaving much more smoothly and
nly in the future. I know that you try not to think about it and
onder if you can just as easily choose to forget those old
omfortable feelings, and your mind can choose only the most
asant things to remember and everything else you can forget to
nk about.

Your memory is always forgetting oversights what it has got
r and done with and you can forget all of the discomfort and
fusion and remembering to be calm and relaxed merely

---

seeing thorns all over the place, he began to count them and certain that he could no longer abide them he removed them all. He worked so frenziedly, he didn't notice the sun shining, or the beautiful smell of the flowers or the colours or even when the sky clouded and began to rain. That night he went home shattered and exhausted but certain that he had removed all the thorns from each plant.

When his wife looked at him she enquired as to what the matter was and when he told her she simply said "this obsession will not do your health any good." The next day (which I think was a Thursday), the gardener returned to work, horrified to discover that every rose bush and plant had begun to re-grow its thorns. At a loss, the gardener made a conscious decision to ignore the thorns. He said to himself "Don't look at the thorns, don't touch the thorns, I will not get cut or scratched by these thorns." Yet despite his thoughts and efforts the gardener became even more cut and scratched than he had ever been in all of his working life. As he sat down in despair looking down at his hands and how bad they appeared to look, a magician who had been watching the gardener for sometime came to offer some advice.

The gardener told the magician all about the thorns and how he just couldn't seem to get rid of the problem because the thorns kept on growing and how when he'd said to himself in his head "Don't look at the thorns, don't touch the thorns, I will not get cut or scratched by the thorns," that he had become more cut and scratched than ever before.

So the magician explained that in life you get more of what you focus on and the gardener said - "I wasn't focusing on the thorns, I was telling myself not to!" So the magician said, "Don't look at the thorns" presupposes that there are thorns and that you can see them and touch them. 'I will not get cut or scratched by the thorns presupposes that not only are there thorns, but they have the ability to cut and scratch you."

"So what is the solution? The solution is to focus on what you *do* want more of - <u>have you noticed the scent of the flowers today, or the new bud over there - just opening, or the cool breeze, or the sound of the children playing?</u>" The gardener had not noticed any of these things.

He said "No, I've been too busy thinking about -" And at that point the magician cast a spell. He didn't magic away all of the thorns, he didn't make them invisible either the problem was still there, a natural problem, <u>there for a good reason</u>. What the magician did was quite simply to make the gardener focus only on the most beautiful elements of the roses, the smells, the colours, and the feel of the velvety petals.

And what happened is the focus became the reality and <u>the problems that were no longer focused on, were no longer there.</u> So although the gardener couldn't make the thorns go away, he learned not to focus on them and focus instead on all of the good and wonderful things. <u>His beliefs became his reality so now there is no pain and only love and roses.</u>

Metaphor for Needle Phobia

Amateur - This is a lovely hypnotic script that uses lots of secret language. When you say particular words to a client in trance, they will not consciously hear the secret language, but unconsciously they will receive the messages you are giving them.

Long, long ago there lived a family community of people who relied on the magical waters of a secret spring, to feel better and to <u>move easily and be injected with goodness and vitality.</u> But the spring was hidden in the depths of a dragon's lair and each new century a townsperson was nominated as the collector of the magical waters.

This century the town folk had nominated a young man called John. Although he appeared quiet and reserved he was a deep thinker and the people had faith that he would be able to come up

with an effective strategy to pass the dragon and magical spring water so desperately needed to ke well.

*(Hypnotherapist say "Needles to say" instead of "Ne Needles to say, in the early days John was not hap prospect of facing a dragon, and having his skin sharp teeth just to get to the magical waters that w body. And after a time he began to really worry w that the injection day was drawing nearer. But th continued to push him and encourage him <u>for his well as their own.</u>

One day John decided not to go to collect the n water, he decided that it really was an unpleasa being scratched and bitten by the dragon and he ju it anymore. The townsfolk were worried and trie him but he refused and became upset and *they* bec more frustrated and in the end they tied him to drove him there themselves. Now you might be a why it is that someone else couldn't have gone and but you see John had been nominated at the turn and would have to continue until the next turn of you can understand why <u>it is important John begir comfortable with the appointments.</u>

When the wagon arrived at the edge of the dr townsfolk untied John and pushed him into struggled and grappled with the dragon, finally s just a small scratch on his arm before the dragon lo allowed him to collect the magical waters from t pass quietly by the dragon back to his village.

For a while, whilst there remained magical wat people well, <u>John didn't even think about the dra</u> the time came when he had only a few days to pr the journey. John became anxious and worried b fortune, a caring relative had sought the assista scratches the surface followed by a smooth and easy feeling. So continue to look inside. Be sure to make all appropriate changes so that you can actually feel yourself *(Hypnotherapist say "be-numbing" instead of "becoming")* be-numbing cooler and so much more free and confident.

Perhaps the calm feeling will spread inside of you like a gentle cool blueness leaving you settled and safe from the inside outwards. The butterflies that once somersaulted can be asked to remain settled and still, enjoying the cool, calmness inside. And as if in a controlled trance you can stride on. You needle-not be concerned with the dragon, just be relaxed and enjoying the gentle blueness as you be-numbing more calm.

As the dragon touches you, remain confident and in control and he will soon know to let you pass quickly, gently scratching past you.

The gentle blueness remains. You are *even now* be-numbing more calm as you make the changes and see yourself being more confident and controlled, knowing that you really will behave that way. Feeling so much better.

Once past the dragon quickly and easily *(Hypnotherapist say "blood-test the water" instead of "test the water")* blood test the water. Feel it injecting vitality and goodness to all of your limbs, joints and every fibre of your being. Then with the same coolness and confidence, finalise any other business and leave.

Be sure that you have made these changes completely and satisfactorily before you head off. You can ask for more of my help if you need it. It only takes a minute and you'll have billions more minutes to spend doing much more interesting things so this is such a tiny fraction of your time that it will all be finished so easily so soon.

Don't give it so much attention. Give the attention to yourself, that lovely cold blue feeling be-numbing more and more. And if you don't behave in that way then I shall make your eyes stay stuck shut until you have agreed to behave in a calm and relaxed way, and they will only open when you are absolutely positive that the changes have been made definitely and completely. And now you have complete confidence that <u>you will behave calmly and coolly</u> and agree to do so in all future appointments from this day on then you shall be able to open your eyes at the end of our chat."

John hadn't even remembered that his eyes were closed and he felt that he had made all of the appropriate changes, which he was able to continue to do as the story progressed, he set about the final steps of the journey to the dragon's cave.

He paid <u>particular attention to his positive thoughts for the future and his deep calm</u>.... He also noticed <u>the gentle tingling as he was be-numbing more at ease.</u> He virtually glided into the cave and was momentarily scratched by the dragon, but <u>it seemed so irrelevant</u>. He collected enough healing water for himself and the people of the village and felt relieved and proud that he had made those changes - <u>making his life so much easier and better, now and in the future</u>. The town's folk were so happy and they felt at ease that they no longer had to worry about John in that instance again.

As John became more unconcerned about the little pricks and scratches it became easier for him to do and to do so more regularly so that his wellness increased more and more until he was able to do just as much as he needed to do.

So when <u>you know John</u>, you can and will do this in exactly the cool and calm way that I have told you, then you will find that you can open your eyes. If there are any further changes that need to be made you will be unable to open them until you have finished making those changes now. So count in your mind from 5-1 and see what happens, see if <u>you have made the changes</u> and can open your eyes when you reach number 1.

Football Metaphor for Phobia.

Amateur - This script is best used after completing the NLP fast phobia cure or as an aid for mild fears, as phobias can be quite intense and may take a little more attention.

Now, I know that you've been dribbling around with the idea of over-coming your phobia, but until now, you haven't had the confidence to strike it out completely.

It is important to always move forwards in life, to advance and progress even if you feel you are a long way back from where you want to be, <u>you have to take control</u>, take the ball by the horns and manoeuvre your way towards your goal. <u>Only you can make you the winner,</u> with your determination and passion to succeed and if you do not push yourself, <u>assert yourself, and overcome your fear,</u> even when you are being pushed to the line, then you will be giving away control.

Here there is a conflict, a match of wills with only one winner, and in order to win you must tackle your way through, even if you're anxious, even when you want to pass the opportunity, <u>keep tackling it and advancing toward the goal. You will always be safe, you can always keep it calm,</u> you are always the one in control because this match is yours, <u>your own to be won</u> and at any time there is any foul play from that old phobia, you can be the referee.

You can keep it in check, show it the red card when it's pushing its luck and when <u>you're ready,</u> when you see that it serves no purpose, only as an obstacle that makes you work harder, draining you of your energy and challenging you, when <u>you're ready send it off.</u> This is your pitch, it has no right to be here. With all of your useful skills and resources working in your mind as a dream team, you do not need to have opposition in your own mind. It's your pitch, you're the referee, send it off.

And then <u>advance forward toward the goal,</u> undeterred by any remaining keeper of your problem. And any adrenalin you feel is that of a wo/man who can smell her/his success in the air, enjoying the journey, taking in the sights and sounds and moments as s/he focused on reaching the goal. <u>And then you are there</u>, and you are full of it and each time you exercise it you become greater <u>and the phobia recedes, you are beating it.</u>

And what trophies will you see in these wonderful new situations, when you are the winner what wonderful experience will await you that would never have been possible before, <u>what will you do now you can? What won't you do now you can?</u> How green the grass really is and what rewards salute your perseverance.

<u>You're in a new league now</u> and you coach yourself evermore, to achieve even more, certain now of your capabilities, eager to kick off and prove your talent and ability.

No more sitting on the bench, <u>just onward now and involved and taking control and matching up to that old phobia, you know you can do this,</u> This is your life and you've got no time to play games so you get on with it, sure of your ability, certain of your control, ready to strike, and really wanting to win and to do it now!

Fear of going out
Amateur - This script aids the client by getting him/her to focus his/her attention outside of himself/herself, instead of on his/her own inner anxieties.

Now I want to speak to you about how you are able to change the way you feel when it is time to go out. You might be wondering <u>how easy this really is</u> but let me tell you that this is something you will be able to learn Sunday *(say as if you are saying Someday)*. I know this because I know that you have one of those mind's that learns quickly and never forgets. I know this because you have told me about that old problem you had about going out, and I know that you learned to do that problem very quickly and you never, in the past, forgot to do it.

Now the things you do in your mind and with your body are going to be directly responsible for your new behaviour. <u>This is very important</u> - you have paid me a lot of money to be here and we have both invested our time and effort into this, so it is very important that in order <u>for this to work totally and completely, you must do exactly the things that I tell you.</u> Add nothing and take nothing away. <u>Do only exactly as I tell you every single time.</u>

The reason you will find this instruction so simple to follow is because there are only a few steps you will take to achieve your desired result. So firstly, I want you to remember that it is only you who is in charge of your thoughts and feelings, that the responsibility for this working lies with you because when <u>you do exactly as I tell you to do it and add nothing and take nothing away</u> you will only be able to go out feeling happy and confident every single time.

The next time you go out, I want you to <u>become very curious</u> about the environment and notice the colour (say the clients favourite colour) in as many places as possible, <u>keep looking for it</u> and every time you see it, <u>acknowledge it by smiling</u>. And every time you smile, <u>remember a time in the past when you felt confident</u> - I mean *really* confident. And I want you to focus on how often you need to blink. Do you blink just once at a time or in two's? Perhaps <u>you can notice how your eyelashes feel as they flutter against your brow bone</u>. Whilst you focus on your blinking rate, I also want you to observe whether you are able to <u>be aware of all of your toes in your shoes and how they are feeling and how comfortable they are.</u> Make sure you <u>stand/sit up straight as you do this.</u> The only thing you have to say to yourself in your mind every time is <u>"I will settle down here. I will settle down here."</u>

So, to recap: Notice the colour and smile every time you see it.

When you smile remember a time in the past when you felt confident.

Focus on your blinking rate.

Be aware of all your toes.

Stand/sit up straight.

Say inside "I will settle down here."

This is your success formula. Add nothing, take nothing away.

That old problem no longer serves you. <u>It's time to let go of it.</u>

~

Bad Habits

~

Nail Biting

Amateur - The first scene in this script can be adapted for those who do not have children, or can be used as a leverage technique if their child has already copied the bad habit. The hypnotherapist could point out that when the child gets sick, he/she may do so because of the germs under his/her fingernails, therefore indirectly applying guilt to the nail biting parent. For extra power, you can add that when the client puts their fingers in their mouth in future, they will feel as if they want to vomit, as if they have stuffed all of their fingers in their mouth, causing them to reach and gag.

And as you continue to <u>drift into a deeper state of relaxation</u>, I would like you to know that all of the suggestions I give you today are for your own benefit and well-being. So I would like you now to make any internal agreement with the part of yourself responsible for decision-making - <u>agree to listen, remember and act or respond in the way that best reflects your interests.</u> Therefore if you hear some directions or instructions related to your nail biting habit, then I would like you to agree now to follow these directions or instructions as they will be for your best interests.

I'm going to ask you now to picture certain things in your mind, and as you do so, I would like you to really notice how these scenes and pictures make you feel, where those feelings start inside of you and perhaps to name these feelings, so that you can create a quick reference to them, whenever you need them.

In NLP, we call this an anchor. Your anchor will be the word, and whenever you think of the word you will be reminded of the picture and the feeling. So let us begin. And the first I would like you to create is this. I want you to imagine that your child has started to bite her/his nails. You notice him/her doing it whilst he/she is watching TV, <u>really chomping away at them</u>, almost unconsciously and quite intensely. I don't want you to think about how you feel too much but you might start to <u>notice that your</u>

heart is beating a bit faster and your breathing has become shallow. There's probably some tension in your body, and you might even want to shout, "stop!"

But you know from your own experience that shouting and nagging rarely result in breaking a bad habit. You know that the way to overcome this is to remain calm and relaxed and just approach him/her and ask why he/she is biting his/her nails. And when he/she replies "but you do it mummy/daddy", then you might start to think about how that makes you feel. Perhaps you can explain to him/her that it makes your fingers really sore and painful. If you can remember the most sore and painful they have ever been then you can picture yourself explaining this and think of the types of words that you will use to explain it to your child.

You might tell him/her about all of the germs and nasties that live under fingernails and on fingers. Ask your child if he/she remembers a time when they felt poorly and you could explain that germs and nasties make us feel poorly and so you really do not want to put your fingers into your mouth.

And if you find that as you stare into the eyes of your child that he/she is really not looking convinced about your reasons to stop, perhaps you could try to explain to them how miserable and embarrassed and ashamed it has made you. You could show him/her your scruffy hands and tell him/her how disappointed in yourself it makes you. Tell this to your child and perhaps as you do, you would listen to your own voice as if you are communicating to the inner child within you.

Make sure you are being as persuasive as you possibly can - and really notice how this makes you feel. Think of the word that you can use to remember this scene and these feelings. Say whatever it is that you need to say to change that bad habit and do it now.

PAUSE

The next scene I would like you to imagine is of yourself, somewhere comfortable and familiar. See if you can picture yourself there as if you are looking through your eyes from inside of your body. Now look down at your hands and see that you have long, strong, natural nails, not false ones, but your own, (without any nail polish), just natural and neat. Not too long, either oval or square tips with the skin around the nail, healthy and the cuticles pushed back, clean and clear - and notice how that makes you feel.

You will probably feel so proud that you just want to keep looking at them, examining them, really satisfied with yourself. Look at your beautiful hands and think of your anchor word to describe this picture and feeling, think of the picture, the feeling and the word. Now, put one of these lovely long nails to your mouth and as you bite it, <u>think about how ridiculous that one finger will look</u> compared to the rest, how <u>self conscious you will be of that one finger, how sore it will be</u>, how you will have to hide it away.

Then take it out of your mouth and look at it. Look at it compared to all the rest of your fingers and notice how bald it looks. Why did you do that? Think of that image. The feeling and the word to describe it, do this over and over again, and as you do so, you will begin to lose any satisfaction that you had when biting your nails, replacing this satisfaction with those feelings of disappointment.

And I wonder how <u>you will avoid that disappointment in the future to create those long nails of the future.</u> The last thing I would like you to imagine is a feeling of certainty. You may have experience a feeling of certainty about something in the past that you can imagine now, or perhaps there are things that you are certain about everyday -that the sun will rise, or certain of your own name. Look down at your own hands with neat tidy nails, not too long, as they are still growing and remember that feeling of certainty.

And as I ask the following questions, continue to look down at your own hands, moving them and touching your nails and answer the following questions with that feeling of certainty inside of you. If you need to enhance that feeling of certainty you can do so by giving the feeling a colour, and making the colour brighter or perhaps you can make the sound of your internal voice stronger and louder, and answer inwardly to yourself:

Will you stop biting your nails?

Answer stronger and more sure inside your mind.

Will you stop?

Will you stop now?

Answer stronger and be surer. Remember the feeling of certainty.

Will you stop now?

Why will you stop now?

Will you put your fingers in your mouth to bite your nails?

Will you ever bite your nails again?

Who do you make this promise to?

Know now that the decision to continue or stop is yours.

If you decide to stop, then you must commit wholly and completely to this, but if you break this promise to yourself you will only be hurting yourself and <u>now is the time to stop doing that.</u> <u>Stop doing it now,</u> and tell yourself with absolute certainty.

"This habit is no longer part of my life. I stop biting my nails, from now; this is my promise to myself."

Nail biting - reducing habits

Amateur - this script brings the old habit into conscious awareness to give the client the opportunity to decide to continue with the behaviour or not. It also integrates an NLP Swish Pattern.

And as you continue to drift and dream and relax, completely and deeply now I want to congratulate the commitment you have made to yourself to leave that destructive habit in your past. Know now that this change is already occurring, you are nearing the light at the end of the tunnel, your commitment will ensure that you are successful in your task.

So for now, all you need to do is lie back, more deeply relaxed than before and look forward now as I guide you towards the future you have to enjoy. What would be your greatest reward from overcoming this dirty habit? Perhaps the long strong natural nails, or would it be moving away from the sore untidy fingers? It might be the relief to scratch an itch with something more than a stubbly finger, or just to know that you are free from the automatic response to put your fingers to your mouth in different situations, or are you looking forward to pampering yourself and painting your nails or to simply no longer feel the need to hide them away, embarrassed at the destruction you caused yourself.

I suspect that your reasons for abandoning that old habit are a combination of all those things. And the beauty is the more you focus on the long term rewards - long, strong, healthy natural nails, the more you train your mind to accept this as your new reality. And the more and more you refuse to partake in that old habit the less and less and less you will experience sore, untidy fingers, embarrassment, no longer a slave to an automatic habit questioning, consciously each time you catch yourself in a situation where you would have to bitten your nails in the past, stopping yourself so that the habit continues to loosen its grip on you, making you free in your choices - whether you do, or whether you don't you decide.

I wonder how overcoming this habit will boost your self-esteem and self-image. Who do you imagine you will become? Standing taller, shoulders back, smiling, shaking hands with someone new, trying on new watches, rings or bracelets and staring down at your hands, seeing your hands confidently pushing open new doors. See an image clearly in your mind of who you will become and when you have taken a few moments to try out that new body and you are satisfied that it is just as you aspire to become, put the image into the corner of a screen in your mind. Then fill the rest of the screen with the image of the habit, of how you used to be and feel. It may be an image of your whole self, or of just your hands. Now slowly begin to drain the colour out of that image until it is almost black and white. If there are any sounds with this image, then turn down the volume, or distance the tone, make this picture seem insignificant and less offensive, then very quickly, sweep the image of your new future self from the corner into the entire screen, eliminating completely that old habit. Do it now as quickly as *SWISH*. **Repeat this paragraph 10 times.**

Look now at who you have the potential to be, who you will become. Compare that person to the person who used to be embarrassed by the appearance of his/her hands. <u>Who do you aspire to become</u>? Surly the answer must be that confident person with the beautiful hands, free from restricting habits. This image completely devalues any <u>short-term</u> pleasure you had ever experienced from that old habit. <u>How would you like some more long term, permanent happiness in place of that old habit?</u>

It is said that old habits derive from pleasure or comfort; however this is often lost when the habit becomes destructive so <u>you no longer even experience pleasure or comfort - only destruction.</u>

From now on, if you should sense any urge to bite your nails I want you to pinch the end of the finger you have the urge to bite, as hard as you can, with you middle finger and thumb of your other hand. This pinch will serve to remind you of the discomfort and destruction of the habit you once had. Choose to do this instead of putting your fingers to your mouth so that you are always consciously aware of your hands drawing near to your mouth. If consciously aware, you decide to undertake that old destructive habit due to tension, or snags and splits in your nails, or uneven edges or any other rubbish excuses you can create for yourself then you do so out of conscious desire and not through habit. <u>The habit has gone and you now have conscious awareness which is a different matter completely.</u>

Did I also mention that whenever you pinch your finger instead of biting your nail that this will also be a trigger to remember that image of you, confident and with beautiful hands - remember her/him?

(Optional)

And perhaps when you are starting to see the evidence of your success, you can treat yourself to reward that success. A pleasant smelling hand cream or a favourite colour nail varnish - it's up to you - I'm sure there are plenty of things you can create for yourself, to reward your success for yourself - so much to look forward to . . . .

OCD (Obsessive Compulsive Disorder)

Professional - Read through the script completely once first so that you can customize the suggestions for your particular client. This script gradually encourages the client to stop their OCD behaviour by reducing the number of things they can obsess about over a series of weeks.

Now feel comfortable, relaxed and secure. You can go back to a time when you felt most restful and open to feeling free.

And as you enjoy this time, the fun of just letting yourself drift, know that everyone is safe in your thoughts and you can invest in peace of mind.

You've got all the time in the world, you're fully safe and secure, so let go.

I know that there's much more in life that you want to be able to do, and it's good to know that you can learn. You can learn just as easily as you learned when you were a child. A carefree happy child....you loved to run, discover and play, with not enough time in the day to do all that you wanted to do, always skipping from one activity to the next with things so easily forgotten. Totally carefree. Do you remember how easily you could be that way?

You were always looking for an adventure, leaving things

incomplete… there was always something much more interesting going on elsewhere, and it didn't matter to you if you forgot to put away all of your toy cars, or to tidy your jigsaw puzzle or to put on your socks, you knew those things will still be there when you get back. And it was easy to just run out of the door without even considering all of the things you needed to do. Then your parents would be saying what about this? What about that? Did you remember to shut the door and to make your bed and to clean your teeth? And you hadn't done these things, it's so easy to forget and feel completely ok. There was a time like this for you, not so long ago and life was so much easier then.

Now we do not ever know what is going to become of us in the future, so it would be true to say that you definitely have the potential to return to that time now in your mind. To be able to feel now, or in the future, all of the carefree feelings and attitudes that you felt then. Only then it was completely natural to feel that way, and now it might take a little bit of gentle practice in order to rediscover the ease at which you can function now. Gentle practice is very beneficial and you can also really enjoy it. Did you know that when you imagine doing something in your mind, the same areas of your brain light up, just as if you were running the strategy in real life? So you can start here, now, by imagining yourself doing all of the things you want to achieve. Imagine yourself now in your mind leaving the house and checking just once that the door is properly secure and then happily going on your way.

Checking just once and feeling happy and confident and free and knowing that everyone is fully safe and secure. Keep repeating these things, imagining over and over with the comfortable feeling that goes with them, and see them again, every time you notice a flicker of colour after you wake. Imagining in this way is practising for success. Therefore, if you would like to be successful in overcoming your sticky situation, you must keep imagining your success for the near future. The other thing you must do is to understand that the checking doesn't control you. <u>You do it, you check, therefore you control the checking, you decide to do it or not to do it.</u>

Not much in life is controllable, but <u>you do have the ability to control your thoughts and emotions and behaviour.</u> The next thing I want you to do is to choose one thing to be completely carefree about the next two weeks, it might be that you're carefree about securing the house or your car or perhaps about the cleaning.

When I say carefree, <u>I mean that you relax enough to check it once only and then be convinced that everything is ok.</u> You can still check everything else you used to check, I think you'll find them still there, <u>but this one thing you will completely relax about.</u> So decide now, in your mind which thing you are going to be carefree about, and do your imaging so that you see yourself being carefree about this thing in a really easy and happy way.

Keep replaying that image over and over again so that it becomes completely natural to you and an integral part of your very being.

Now tomorrow when you start this carefree way about only this one thing or thought if you like, it might feel as if you're going against the grain a bit. But it's ok because you can still check all of the other things just as much. <u>Only checking this one thing will have stopped.</u> All of the others can stay the same.

Sometimes when we do something in a new way or a new place, it's a bit odd at first, a bit going against the grain. Just as when you were little and you went from your junior school to your senior school, it was a bit different, a bit odd and there were new rules to learn, <u>but you adjusted soon enough and were very comfortable there and after a short time being there, it seemed like the normal place to be.</u>

It felt a bit like going against the grain but everything else remained the <u>same and you were soon able to grow in this new direction, and it only takes two weeks -</u> that's all, just two weeks, for these new comfortable feelings to happen automatically, until they happen automatically, you'll have to pretend you have them in your imaginings.

The first three days will feel particularly strange, but if you can manage those, then you move onto the next four days. Once you've got those out of the way, you've done a week already.

Days 8-11 might seem impossible, so remember to use your imaginings vividly and then you will have enough momentum to do days 12-14.

After day 14 you'll be fine, it'll feel normal not to check one thing by then. I know you like a challenge, which is probably why you set this for yourself. I have this friend who hates to be challenged in anyway. I always like to know what I'm capable of achieving; after all we've been given these bodies and thoughts for a reason.

Why waste them?

Make the most of them.

Lying

Amateur - This script gives the client the opportunity to evaluate their reasons for lying. In doing so they have the option to reassess their decisions and consider changing their behaviour.

Now, I'm going to be honest with you, there are a number of reasons why people lie. But isn't it interesting - the first reason is fear. This is the most common reason. Now you may think that perhaps the fear is of being found out that you've been doing something you shouldn't have been doing - but this isn't the case. The purpose of a lie is to give you shelter from a perceived punishment - to lock yourself away from the punishment, but haven't you kept the truth locked up for a while now? You really do not need to do that to yourself anymore.

You no longer need to fear a punishment, because from now on you are going to begin to understand more about why you lie, which will cause you <u>to interrupt the construction of a lie before it leaves your mouth.</u> It's time to step out into the open now, no more locking yourself away, no more skeletons in closets, <u>open, free, and honest.</u>

There remain two further reasons why a person may continue to lie even after eradicating the habit of lying and even after stopping the self-punishment. Another reason why is when you have learned to lie because you have watched others lying and have seen them get away with it. If this is the case then just ask yourself - Do <u>you want to become like that person, is this someone you could aspire to be?</u> Or should you <u>start now doing everything possible to be better than that</u> - a better husband/wife, father/mother, friend, colleague - <u>a better friend to yourself?</u>

The last reason why people lie is because they feel that if they tell the truth, they wouldn't get what they want. I wonder what kind of person you would become if you were always to get what you wanted. Consider children - what might their behaviour be like if you always gave them everything they wanted- as a parent to yourself, you know that always getting what you want is quite corrupting, that as individuals we need to earn things to truly give them value and meaning.

And now you have much to earn - <u>you need to earn back your respect</u>, but before you can get it from others, you need to have it within yourself, for yourself.

Stop Evening Drinking Habits

Amateur - This script is used for a client who uses alcohol in the evenings to ensure that they unwind and have a good night's sleep.

As you <u>continue now to relax rest back very comfortably.</u> Notice the sensations in your body, how <u>deeply relaxed you are by breathing easily and comfortably and deeply.</u> Noticing for example that the sensations are different when you breathe in and when you breathe out. Notice these feelings as you breathe in and fill your lungs and notice the sense of <u>release as you breath out</u>. <u>Releasing, relaxing and letting go completely</u>. Teetering on the edge of <u>complete and deep restful sleep</u>. Knowing that your body is able to <u>access this state of deep relaxation</u> simply by noticing your breathing, whether it is for relaxation or in order to aid your gentle <u>slip into a deep and restful night's sleep. L</u>et your mind wander only to the most peaceful places and relax deeper and deeper.

Giving up alcohol in favour of relaxation will only reap positive physical benefits: <u>a deep and natural sleep, undisturbed and still;</u> waking with a clear head, bright and refreshed in the morning.

As you <u>continue to experience that deeply relaxed trance,</u> knowing that <u>you will experience this natural relaxation</u> whenever you wish, with the only tool for doing so being your own breathing and silenced thoughts, I want to talk to yourself in the way that feels most appropriate for you. And I want to talk to that aspect of your mind that is most concerned in hearing, what I have to say; that is most interested in helping you to get the outcome that you want.

And you know what you want and that is why you are here today. To make changes that will benefit your health and wellbeing. And sometimes it can be just as if we are stuck in a bad habit and can see what might be right or better for us but give so much attention to what we are doing wrong it becomes difficult to change when really change can be as simple as flicking a switch inside our minds to enable us to switch our behaviour. People think that the mind is a very complex tool and they would be right, but <u>some things work very easily and simply and to switch our behaviour is a very easy thing to do.</u>

Just let yourself know, almost as if you are sending a kind of signal through your mind, a signal of clarity, in which you acknowledge that you are clear about the fact, that <u>you now have no anxiety</u>. That you are thoroughly interested and willing, with full intention, to carry out this plan, <u>to relax, completely independently without the use of anything other than your mind.</u> And if all that your mind requires is permission to change your old habit to a new, healthier and rewarding one then please do <u>give that permission to your mind now.</u>

Have you noticed how <u>peaceful and easy it is to relax there,</u> now, <u>deeper and deeper</u> with each passing minute which seems to slow down with every word you hear? Isn't it so wonderful to feel such total relaxation and yet knowing that <u>you are completely safe and in complete control of yourself and the situation around you.</u> This is not the case if you have been drinking alcohol, no matter how acquired you are, you will never be as in control as you would be if you were completely sober. And of course you may if you wish, have the occasional glass of wine of an evening as we know that it can be safe, even beneficial to do so.

You know that you need not drink the entire bottle and if you suspect that you would, you know not to have any at all that day. <u>Simply use the time that you would have attended to your wine on better things.</u> You may like to spend more time with your family or friends, perhaps take up a hobby that you have never got round to doing or perhaps going swimming or to the gym. You know that <u>there are better ways to treat your mind and body.</u>

So picture yourself now, leaving work after a particularly hard day. As you walk out through the doors to the outside, move any stresses or worries from your day to the back of your mind. Imagine them or gauge the way each stress or worry makes you feel and lock them away into storage in the back of your mind, ready to deal with the following day<u>. If you do want to discuss any aspect of your day you can do so with ease,</u> feeling unaffected as you do not let your stresses interfere with your relaxation. Imagine your journey home. You can begin to plan the start of your evening on your journey home, thinking what food you will prepare and eat, what you may like to watch on T.V., or if you will be meeting friends instead, perhaps you will discuss the family holiday or the plans for a relative's birthday party.

You get home and are contently busy with things. When you do <u>sit down to completely relax,</u> you are surprised at <u>how easily this is achieved,</u> just by focusing your mind a little and taking some slow deep breaths <u>you soon feel the same level of relaxation that you are experiencing here, now.</u>

As the evening progresses you notice your body's cues for sleep. You know not to ignore these and prepare a glass of water to take up to bed. You know that you need to undress, wash and brush your teeth but it all seems such an effort - <u>you have become so relaxed.</u> You motivate yourself to do so on the promise that you will soon be relaxed in your cosy bed, and this enables you to prepare yourself quickly, until in bed.

Notice how completely relaxed you feel now. Know that this is achieved in just a few moments of lying still and focusing on your breathing. When your body is ready, you will sink down deeper and deeper into that still deep and restful sleep, until you wake refreshed and revived. Feeling so proud and surprised each morning as you realise that the night before, it didn't even cross your mind to drink a bottle of wine to get you off to sleep. <u>You coped perfectly well without it </u>as if <u>that old problem is forgotten completely.</u>

~

Addictions

~

Split Road Drug Addiction

Professional - I first used this script with a client who had a heroin addiction and it provided the Turning Point in his recovery. Get the client to share some ideas about the future with you prior to using this script so that they are able to fully engage in the process.

Throughout this trance you will be able to speak to me without being disturbed from this peaceful state.

As you continue to rest so comfortably there, <u>enjoying this restful sleep</u>, balancing on the edge of total, complete, deep sleep <u>that you will enjoy experiencing when you go to bed later and each night until the next time I see you and relaxing now twice as much each time you hear me say deeper and deeper</u>.

See before you now, a road which splits in two. Notice the area where you stand, it is a peaceful quiet place that enables you to relax now, deeper and deeper, as you know that this road is free from traffic and you are able to listen to the sounds in nature, the birds in the background, the breeze brushing gently through the grass, all helping you to relax deeper and deeper now.

If you look to where the road splits to the right, this represents to you the way your life will go in the future, free from addiction, sharing a good life with others. The path looks bright, sunny, well lit and open. The air feels fresh and warm and the thought of this road creates a feeling of <u>comfort, freedom and love inside of you</u>.

Think now of the wonderful events that will occur in your future to enable you to <u>experience feelings of comfort, freedom and love.</u>

Immerse yourself in how comfort will feel, what image it creates and the things that you might hear or will be said to you when you experience comfort in your future. And what of freedom?

Just imagine <u>how it will feel to be free in your future,</u> what picture does freedom show you? Notice the feelings inside you - where it begins and grows stretching out to each fibre in your body. Focus now, on what you will hear, what people may say to you that tells you - you have freedom now.

And now as you look down that road, you know that in your future there will be love. Love may come to you now as a strong feeling moving through you and around you, securing you in a bubble. You will vividly hear from your family and friends words of love, sharing your life and your future with those who love and care for you. See those who love you on this road, those who are already in your life who love you now, and those you have yet to meet. Start to walk down this road now and look at this road, your future, through your own eyes.

Look further down this road to a scene in the future in two months time. You feel completely free of any addictions, because you associate a life without drugs and excessive alcohol, as a successful life. You know that living without the dangerous and harmful substances brings happiness and success in abundance.

Look at where you are. As you walk through your house, go to a room where you can catch your reflection and notice how much fitter and stronger you look. There is a healthy glow in your in your skin, you stand still and look relaxed and happy. Your happiness sweeps over you as you reflect on the interesting weeks work you have been completely engaged in, and think of the tasks you look forward to finishing.

Notice those around you and become aware of the way they think and feel about you. You may be aware of how proud they have become and how much more they value you as a person. When you think back to the addiction you used to have, you feel immense relief that it no longer has a hold on you. So much so, you realise that the thought hadn't bothered you for a long-time. It was as if you took that nagging voice and turned the volume down more and more, each day you wake turn down the volume until the nagging addiction is shut up and silent.

You take a deep breath and look to your reflection again. Notice the expression on your face, how will you look when you achieve <u>and are feeling so proud that you have done so.</u> Make the colours in what you see brighter and clearer, hear the sounds around you in stereo and notice every good feeling inside of you, where they begin and encourage the feeling to grow then immerse yourself in them. Totally in control.

Move back to the road now and wander a little further to a scene in eight months time. You have been working extra hard to save money. You are looking forward to having your own space and spending your time making it happen. You feel excitement as you spend some time with a family member and your mind is flooded with ideas and inspiration. You may sense that your relatives feel a little anxious but you are able to give them total reassurance as you feel confident that your life is moving forward in the most positive and fortunate direction. You remind them that <u>you are where you are today as a result of changing for the better and that you have absolutely no intention of doing the destructive things you had done in your past.</u> Think now of how you will say this and really turn up the level of confidence you have in what you say. Have complete confidence and conviction, because you know that it is true. (Pause)

Move back to the road and travel further into the future, you notice that the road slopes upwards slightly. It can be hard work walking this road but it has the best opportunities to offer. Stop at a scene one year from today, and immerse yourself into this scene, the feelings, the colours and the sounds. In the scene you are with <u>someone whom you feel great love for</u>. You may not yet know this person so don't worry if you cannot see every detail of them, but just know that they are there, enjoying your company and that you share a great love for each other with complete trust. You love this person more because of the total trust they have in you. Imagine how you will feel with this person when you care for them so dearly, you love to be close to them. Perhaps you are in a new environment, perhaps you are discussing the future with this person, it may be about your future together or perhaps a business venture you can plan together. Notice the furniture in the room, the smells and the sounds from outside.

(Pause)

Move back to the road and travel six years into the future. It is your birthday and you are spending the day with your whole family. There may be family members who are there who you have yet to meet; perhaps they are your future children. If you cannot focus on their faces at this stage, do not worry - they will all be beautiful.

Your family are there to congratulate you and celebrate. You listen to the things they say. <u>You have so much to be proud of</u>. When you look back on how your life has changed and when you think of that person you have become you think "I'm a good person with good friends, I'm having such a good life I can't stop smiling!"

And when you think of your past, you know that there was a positive purpose to your experience - you will protect and educate others at the right time, to make sure that they do not make the mistakes that you made in your past. <u>You feel strongly and passionately about it, the purpose of that past experience.</u>

And now I will give you a few moments to enjoy your future, think about the things you have to look forward now and into your future, think of good experiences and take a few moments to enjoy a whole day, go there, be there now (Pause).

Tell me one word that describes this life. ....

Now, I would like to take you back to the road at the point of today. You will see that as well as the road you have just experienced, there is another road, going in the opposite direction. You have the option to take this road instead of the experience you have just had. Look at this road - it is much shorter and darker, there is almost nothing there, it is silent and cold. On this road you have kept and even developed your bad habits. Move towards the road now and as you do so, take a deep breath in through your nose, notice the stale sickly smell in the air travelling to your lungs making you nauseous.

You walk with slow and weak steps to a scene six months into your future. You observe yourself in this scene as if you are watching a film at the cinema, taking in all of the details. You see yourself at home, you are home because you lost your job, you partly overslept. It's true, on a number of occasions; but also felt that you just couldn't do it. You knew that you were on the slippery slope to wasting away and you didn't stop it. You didn't want to try anymore.

Now you just try to lose the day before you go off in the evening to get yourself a fix. Imagine seeing yourself there walk into the room, right up to this *(client's name)*, who is sat in the chair, perhaps shaking. The air is thick and chocking through the smoke, you catch a whiff of the cigarette butts in the ashtray/ stench of an unclean home and it makes you feel sick from your stomach up to your throat. Look at *(client's name)* face, it is so white, he/she looks ill, there are dark circles around his/her eyes. He/she is tense and fidgets a lot, his/her breaths shallow and he/she is hunched over. You can tell that he/she is only thinking of one thing, the only thing left in his/her life. His/her expression is anxious and irritated. He/she is feeling really depressed and his/her body is at a physical low - his/her mouth and lips covered in ulcers that sting each time he/she drags on a cigarette (joint)/ has a drink.

He/she has a general sickness like a pressure on his/her chest and he/she is short of breath. Sometimes he/she wonders how his/her life could have been different, but these thoughts made him/her feel worse so they are quickly replaced.

Move back to the road now, and travel a further two months, you notice a scene where *(client's name)* is no longer at home, s/he is carrying a bag of clothes as he has been kicked out of his/her home. The habits (heroin, cocaine etc..) was costing more and more because he/she needed more and more but he/she didn't have any money. He/she had sold his/her belongings to raise some cash and sent him/her crazy, until he/she sold everything he/she ever owned, even the right to live in his/her own place. He/she thoughts he/she would stay with friends but he/she needed a (fix, line, puff, pill etc) first. And he/she has the money so he/she goes to get *(substance client is addicted to)*. This one is different because you see, everyday, he/she needs more and more for it to have any impact and he/she is so angry, he needs it to work fast so today s/he might use a needle. S/He has pain in every part of his body, it starts as dull toothache all across the bottom teeth and then seems to envelop s/his entire head, his/her limbs feel heavy and there is pain in every bone, more and more.

Move back to the road, and go to the scene one step before the end of the road. You will see yourself in a hospital bed. There are wires all over you and a drip and heart monitor beside you. This *(client's name)* is awake and conscious with his/her family around him/her. They have come to see him/her for the last time. They know this is the last time because he/she had to be resuscitated last night, *(client's name)* heart is failing and s/he still doesn't know if he/she is HIV positive because the blood test results haven't come back yet.

(Client's name) is thin, you see he/she is so scared, so bad, in such pain all over his/her body aching and cramping. His/her face is hollowed, his/her eyes bloodshot and dark. His/her teeth are grey, his/her lips dry and cracked. He/she is confused, sick and crying.

Now I want you to step into this *(client's name)*, be him/her now, staring out at your family around you, feel your mother's (or whoever) tears drip onto your thin hand, the hard tightness in your throat and chest and back. Pain in your head and kidneys, increasing with each breath, making you more uncomfortable. You feel so sick and you need to tell your family now that the next time your heart stops, you do not want it restarted. Tell them now in your sick, weak voice and watch their faces. Now turn up the pain in every part of your body and tell them now.

Is this the future you want?

Tell me one word to describe this life. ....

Now I want you to move back to the road at the point where two futures lay ahead of you, and decide in your own mind the road you will take.

Have you chosen............road or...........? *(refer to the names of the roads the client gave you earlier)*

Today we have set a negative feeling that will occur in your body every time you think about taking *(substance client is addicted to)* in the future. To stop experiencing negative thoughts or feelings you must stop thinking about taking *(substance client is addicted to)* and replace these obsessive thoughts with an obsession to achieve your........(the word they gave to describe the positive life) in the future.

Each time thoughts of *(substance client is addicted to)* come to your mind, replace the thought with something you need to do to make your future brighter. You need not feel angry with yourself for thinking of *(substance client is addicted to)* but praise yourself for the ability to replace the thought with ease as you notice more and more how much less and less frequently you forget to remember *(substance client is addicted to)*.

Drug Reduction Anchors

Professional - This script is used for clients who are on a drug treatment programme (such as a methadone programme) and want to start weaning off the drug to be completely clean.

As you continue to relax further, I'd like you to be aware of the routine you follow on the mornings when you go to collect more (drug rehab treatment substance). You can think of this routine very quickly as you rest comfortably there and you need not be concerned if you do not see every picture clearly or if worry if at times my voice seems to drift and fade as I am now talking to the unconscious part of your mind, the part that is responsible for doing things without your conscious awareness of them happening. In the same way your unconscious mind beats your heart, or makes you blink without you being aware of it happening, you will continue to listen and make changes, at that very level, so do not worry if you drift from the words or instructions, just be absolutely certain that the changes are taking place and have confidence in this.

So see yourself as you get up in the morning and get ready for your appointment, see yourself travelling to the clinic. Go to the door of the clinic now and slowly: do this in slow motion, see yourself lift your hand to the metal door and when I say "now" I want you to see yourself touch the door and think about how that metal door will feel against the skin on your palm and all of the tiny muscles you are using to move that door and its weight. And when you see yourself do that and you think of that metal door, and your hand and the muscles in your hand and your shoulder and your arm, I want you to also think about how you can reduce the amount of (drug rehab treatment substance) you take, and how easily you can discuss this with your drugs councillor.

S/he might suggest a lower dosage, or perhaps taking it on a lesser frequency. So when you are ready, reach the door and as your hand touches it think of reducing the (drug rehab treatment substance) now. And you know that this is a really positive step to take because you will become cleaner and the cleaner you are, the better you feel.

And as you sign in you can think to yourself, "yes, today I will speak to the drugs councillor about reducing the amount of (drug rehab treatment substance) I take." And then you see him/her and talk about how well you are doing and feeling and you say to him/her "Can I reduce the amount of (drug rehab treatment) I take?" and s/he will discuss this with you before printing and signing your prescription. And then you leave and travel to the chemist. As you walk in through the sliding doors you know you are entering into a better future as you feel happy and satisfied that you are reducing the (drug rehab treatment substance), and you chat and laugh with the people in the chemist whilst you wait, feeling as if a weight has been lifted.

And when you take the (drug rehab treatment substance) and that horrible taste is in your mouth you think "Thank goodness I am moving away from these old habits, and my addiction is disappearing," and you find that this only motivates you toward a future of happiness in an effort to move away further from that old life, that past addiction. You want and know that you need to establish a better routine in life for your mind and your body.

Parts Therapy - Dealing with Addictions

Professional- this script is for a client who has spent some time being free of drugs but has felt compelled to start taking them again. You can usually indicate a "parts issue" in a client because they will say things like "part of me want to stop, another part doesn't" "I feel torn apart by this" "Sometimes I can, sometimes I can" or any other statements that presupposes incongruence or fragmentation.

It can now be a relaxing experience to discover that you have been aware all along, that you know the real reason for your addiction that seemed so strong, is overpowered by your commitment and total determination to achieve a life of happiness.

An addiction is much like an obsession and you know that you are able to easily change the strong emotion into a drive and determination to achieve happiness. You will find this an easy task, as you know that emotions can be activated, deactivated or changed in a split second. The way a good movie can draw you in and make you feel real fear, sadness or curiosity and when the movie finishes the emotions are gone, and you are busy thinking and feeling about what you want to do next in your day.

You have proved that you can be clean and you know how much better you feel, how much more real life has become since you have continued to be clean. The addiction which seemed so strong is overcast and overpowered by <u>your determination to</u> <u>achieve happiness</u>. You find it easy to <u>change a strong addiction</u> <u>into a powerful evolving determination to achieve happiness,</u> <u>motivated to undertake tasks and plans to determine a secure and</u> <u>happy future</u> at all of the times when you used to think about drugs. You know that you will turn addiction into a determination to succeed and it will be easy to do, <u>because you are</u> <u>stronger than a habit created by your own mind.</u> You will become increasingly aware of anything harmful that you put into your body. This will happen easily and unconsciously. The less you take, the better you feel, the better you feel, the less you take.

Thinking back now to the negative effect that drugs had on you, <u>you now feel so much, fresher, fitter, alert and alive,</u> why would you want to crave the way you were before? Sometimes there seems to be a part of us which is in conflict with what you consciously know is good and right for you. <u>You consciously</u> <u>know that you will turn addiction into a determination to achieve</u> <u>success and happiness that this is the right thing for you to do,</u> <u>and it can be achieved easily</u>. Yet I accept that there is a part of you that wants still, to take drugs, and this part of you has my respect and deserves yours. It can appear so powerful so now go deep within your own mind searching deeper down, heavier and deeper as you go <u>deeper with every breath</u>. I wonder how quickly you can in the next minute, experience that part which I will call your 'subconscious addiction.'

I do not know how you will experience that addiction part that believes you need to take drugs or what special language will allow you to <u>have communication with that part in a safe and</u> <u>comfortable way</u>. I ask you now to seek the answers to some important questions that you need to understand in order to change addiction into a determination to achieve success and happiness.

Now take some time and go very deep inside to become aware of the pay-offs and benefits that are associated with feeling the addictions? Has the addiction helped you get something that some part of you wanted? You have been clean now for sometime so the addiction is a psychological one and no longer physical. Has the addiction helped you to avoid something uncomfortable or hurtful? Again I am asking you to continue with the assumption that your subconscious addiction has helped you or benefited you in some way. So please become aware of it in a safe and comfortable way. (Pause)

Now keep those pay-off/benefits in mind. Know now that there are alternative ways of experiencing those pay-offs and benefits that the addiction used to provide, alternative ways which are much healthier. <u>Perhaps by using the power of the addiction to fuel a determination to achieve success and happiness.</u>

Please take some time and go inside your mind, as deep as you can reach and allow that part of you which is creative and the part which can solve problems and construct some alternative behaviours that you will easily substitute for that old feeling of addiction and craving that will provide all of those pay-offs and benefits which drugs provide for you in the past.

I want you to take all the time that you need <u>within the next two minutes</u> to check with that part of you and all other parts of you that these new alternatives are acceptable and are seen to be acceptable, sound acceptable and feel acceptable to that part and all other parts of you. If you experience anything which appears to be a 'no' signal, such as an increased tension or irritability in response to the new alternatives you make, you will need to go back inside to find a new acceptable alternative which you may need to find somewhere much deeper down. You might need to take into account some benefits/pay-offs you were not aware of before. Lift a finger to let me know when this process is complete.(Pause).

Please go back into your inner mind now and allow your imagination to show yourself in these times and places where you took drugs in the past. See yourself aware of and utilising your new alternative patterns of behaviour that your creative mind has constructed for you - imagine yourself in these and all other context where you would have felt addiction, now using your new and healthier alternatives. If you experience any difficulty, it may be necessary for you to go back and generate more suitable alternatives. Perhaps you need to take into account some future context that you have just become aware of. Move your finger to indicate to me when you have successfully imagined all future contexts using your new alternatives.

Now I would like you to thank that part of you for its beneficial communication as I now express my thanks also. You may not be consciously aware of the work that has been done but <u>feel completely assured that your subconscious is fully aware and may have even decided to do some work on other habit problems you may have</u>, and you will be pleasantly surprised when you discover that you find it so easy. Now one last thing, we all work better as a whole, instead of being fragments of ourselves. So I would like you to invite all parts of yourself to become integrated into a whole person again. Just like you were in the very beginning. There is much more power in wholeness.

I want to congratulate you on the excellent work you have done and now as you listen to my voice you can find that you can concentrate on that sound, as all other sounds fade into insignificance as you now allow yourself to enjoy the peace and tranquillity of that special place that is yours, relaxed and sinking down, heaviness of arms, legs, body in a pleasantly natural way.

Drugs - After Relapse

Professional - This script utilises the relapse as an opportunity for the client to compare life with and without drugs. This can be more beneficial than the client wallowing in the disappointment of their relapse, which is likely to create further negative feelings and potentially encourage them to numb those feelings by indulging in the drugs again.

And now you can <u>be completely relaxed</u> to know that even the things which occur in life which seem to make little sense to us or make us react in a way that we later question, can hold a great benefit to our future success.

As you <u>look back over the changes you have been making during the past few weeks,</u> you can now see how each moment; each vital piece of information has reinforced the overwhelming commitment and determination inside of you. Even the mistakes you may have made now seem to have <u>had a purpose to remind you of exactly why the changes must remain permanent, conclusive and eternal.</u>

You can now see in your clear and clean state of mind, the difference in your life. The opportunities that are now available to you and will become available to you in your future. The massive and blossoming difference to your health as <u>everyday you grow fitter and fresher, and the clarity and peace of your state of mind.</u> The cloud of depression is dispersing, the fog of fulfilment all being burned away by a bright and positive warm sun <u>that is your own self-worth, confidence and future of happiness.</u>

Everything about you is changing for the better, so fast, so dramatically, so definitely <u>even your tone and vocabulary is uplifted.</u> And now you can see you have been there and back again, back now never to return and choosing to lose the negative emotions and unwanted behaviours as easily as irrelevant thoughts which are lost or forgotten <u>when thinking of something wonderful you could be doing instead.</u>

Letting a sense of comfort, of wellbeing, of confidence, flow through your body like a pleasurable force, <u>so real that you can feel it in your body now.</u> Some people feel it like a colour, or a muscle sense or an inner glow. Each person knows what it is, even though different words are used. It is more than a lack of strain or tension. <u>It is a positive strength that is your own,</u> that can help you learn to recognise it and use it to reduce big challenges into manageable sizes or to eliminate them completely.

As you enjoy that feeling of strength within you, notice the way you are breathing, and know that whenever you want to return to this feeling of strength, you can do it just by taking a few moments to alter your breathing and to breathe the same way as you are breathing now. And with each breath you take it seems to clean and cleanse you, allowing the feeling of strength and well-being to grow.

That determination for success becoming stronger in your subconscious mind with every focused breath you take, making it part of you, making it yours, yours to call on whenever you want it. Should you feel stress building up, breathe those calming breaths of strength and you will be able to put yourself into this trance to draw on your sense of well-being, to, focus on self confidence, reflecting on all you have successfully achieved.

Whatever is troubling you can be brought back to a manageable size, to be dealt with in the most appropriate way. Sometimes in part, little by little if you are not ready to tolerate it all at once. And then you can either continue the trance or terminate it as you deal with the situation effectively.

As you practice with this success feeling, you will become increasingly secure in your ability to cope reasonably, you will be able to live and act appropriately while in any situation.

~

How to Create Excellent
Hypnosis Scripts

~

How to create Excellent Hypnosis Scripts

This part of the book gives hypnotic techniques for creating the very best hypnosis scripts. For each hypnotic pattern, there are examples of how individual sentences can be structured. Words are marked out to give guidance - keywords relating to a sentence structure are underlined, words that need particular emphasis are in bold or italics.

You can use a variety of these techniques in every script you write, though it's a good idea to master the different patterns one by one.

Remember that the unconscious mind does not process negatives (for example if I told you "don't think of the queen" your mind would first have to think of her, then delete the image. Your mind will always have to find and focus on any negative instructions before replacing the thought with something else.) This means that where possible, it's a very good idea to get your clients to focus, whilst in trance, on what they want to achieve instead of what they should not do or should stop doing.

Linguistic Presuppositions

There are certain things that can be presupposed in the sentences we create. Using this knowledge, we can influence the minds of our clients to encourage them to presuppose things that we want them to think about throughout their trance experience.

1. Existence:
- Listen for Nouns. This presupposes that someone or something exists.

  "I know that you're thinking…" (I exist and you exist.)

2. Possibility/Necessity:
- Listen for Modal Operators. These are rule based words such as should, could, can, will, maybe, possibly, shouldn't, couldn't, can't, won't, may not, impossible etc

  "You should be happy, you know you can smile."

3. Cause – Effect:
- Listen for "makes", "if….then", "because" in the sentence. It presupposes that one thing causes another.

  "If you listen to my voice, then you will go into a trance…"

4. Complex Equivalence:
- Listen for "is," "are," "means," "whilst" in the sentence. It presupposes that 2 or more things are happening simultaneously.

  "You are listening and that means you are learning…"

5. Awareness:
- Listen for Verbs relating to the senses.

  "You can hear my voice and feel yourself relaxing more."

6. Time:
- Listen for Verb tense, "stop," "now," "yet."

"<u>Stop</u> <u>now</u>, and listen only to the sound of my voice."

7. Adverb/Adjective:
- Listen for words adding detail to Nouns and Verbs.
  "It is <u>extremely</u> relaxing to breathe <u>deeply</u> in."

8. Exclusive OR/ Inclusive OR:
- Listen for "or".
  Inclusive or- this is when a choice is given that *includes* other options.
  "Would you like to go into a trance or go for a run?"
  Exclusive or- this excludes other options so that only one choice is given, even though it may give the illusion of a choice. The word "only" is also classed as an exclusive or.
  "Would you like to relax a lot or a little?" (Either way relaxation will occur)

9. Ordinal :
- Listen for lists, numbers, orders, sequence.
  "<u>Firstly</u>, I want you to close your eyes, the <u>next thing</u> you will need to do is concentrate."

Putting it all together:

I (<u>Existence</u>) will speak to you now (<u>Time</u>), you can make those changes that you really wish to make, for **you're unconscious** mind is listening (<u>Awareness</u>) and will receive and act upon the messages it hears. And you will find, as this is happening, that you become much happier, within yourself. So much more...delighted with who you are, what you have and everything you can offer.

Can (<u>Possibility</u>) you remember a time where you have felt feelings of confidence, or (<u>Exclusive or</u>) perhaps in a confident time that you've yet to experience? And if you can, remember how you stood. Then you'll know it's very easy to behave in this way

(<u>Cause and effect</u>).

Firstly (<u>Ordinal</u>) think about what you really do want to achieve whilst you're here (<u>Complex Equivalence</u>)....your outcome to be relaxed and at ease now with who you are and all of your amazing (<u>adverb</u>) qualities not to be denied, for you know, it matters not who is judging you, what they might be thinking, you can never really know that and it doesn't matter anyway.

Create a script using at least 8 of the above linguistic presuppositions.

Visit

www.peoplebuilding.co.uk and download one of the free Hypnosis scripts. Establish which linguistic presuppositions occur in the script.

Intonation patterns
In the English Language
The arrows indicate how tone of voice is used in the sentence.

(W= words in the sentence)

W ⟶ W ⟶ **W = Question**

E.g. "Can you relax easily?"

W ⟶ W ⟶ **W = Statement**

E.g. "You can relax easily."

W ⟶ W ⟶ **W = Command**

E.g. "Can you, *relax easily*."

You can also form a sentence in a syntactic pattern (sentence structure) in the form of Question, Statement or Command, while using any of the above tonalities.

By far, the most powerful syntax in the English Language is a Questioning Syntax with a Command Tonality. These are called embedded commands in hypnosis and are extremely powerful for creating positive suggestions for change.

Create 10 everyday questions and re-write them as embedded commands.

Visit

www.peoplebuilding.co.uk and download one of the free Hypnosis scripts. See what embedded commands can be marked out and underline them.

The Milton Model

The Milton Model Utilises Hypnotic Language Patterns. They can be used to create confusion and are very ambiguous. This is a very gentle way to induce a trance experience. It was created from modelling hypnotherapist Milton H. Erickson

1. **Mind Reading:**
    Claiming to know the thoughts or feelings of another person without identifying how you know what they are thinking or feeling.
    "I know that you're wondering..."

2. **Lost Performative:**
    A statement that makes a judgment but does not identify who made the judgment.
    "It's good to enjoy your learning..."

3. **Cause & Effect:**
    A statement that implies that one thing causes another:
    " ...causes...," "If... then...," "As you... then you...," "Whilst...then...," "makes."
    "Because of this course, you will become smarter."

4. **Complex Equivalence:**
    Where two things have the same meaning or are said to be the same. One thing is equal to another.
    "and that means..."

5. **Presuppositions:**
    The equivalent of linguistic assumptions.
    "You are developing your skills..."

6. **Universal Quantifiers:**
    Words that have the following characteristics:

a. Universal generalisations
b. No referential index.
   "Everybody does, all the time."

7. **Modal Operators:**
   Words that imply Possibility/Impossibility or Necessity/ Negative Necessity. They have a tendency to form the rules we have in life.
   "You should find this so easy."

8. **Nominalizations:**
   When a verb has been frozen in time making it into a noun.
   "I'm gaining new insights into our communications."
   (Communicating is something that you *do* where as communications sounds more like a *thing* with form.)

9. **Unspecified Verbs:**
   "Just let go..."

10. **Tag Questions:**
    A closed question added to the end of a statement.
    "Won't you?"

11. **Lack of Referential Index:**
    A statement in which it is not clear *who* the statement refers to.
    "People can learn..."

12. **Comparative Deletions: (Unspecified Comparison)**
    Where a comparison is made but it is not specified against what or whom the comparison was made.
    "You can relax more...."

13. **Pacing Current Experience:**
Undeniably describing the client's internal or external experiences.
   "And as you sit there, blinking, breathing and listening..."

14. **Double Binds:**
Where an illusion of choice is formed but no matter which choice is taken the outcome is the same.
   "Your unconscious..... will make the changes it needs to make instantaneously or maybe even quicker than that." (Whether instant or quick, the changes will occur.)

15. **Conversational Postulate:**
A closed question, which creates an Internal Representation (thought or focus) within the client of something you want them to do. It allows the client to choose to respond or not and avoids authoritarianism.
   "Could you relax more than that?"

16. **Extended Quotes:**
Where it is not possible to detect where one quote finishes and the next one begins.
   "Whilst completing my trainers training, I spoke with Milton Erickson who told me that Fritz Perls mentioned whilst working with Richard Bandler that he had said "Learning NLP can be such great fun."

17. **Selectional Restriction Violation:**
A sentence which gives human-like characteristics to inorganic objects or things.
   "What do your actions tell you?"

18. **Ambiguities:**
    Phonological:
    Where two words sound the same but have different meanings.
    Here/Hear.
    There/Their/They're.
    Peace/Piece.
    Would/Wood.
    Syntactic:
    Where the function of a word cannot be immediately determined from the immediate context.
    "Frying pans can be expensive."
    Scope:
    Where it cannot be identified to which portion of a sentence a word applies.
    "Relaxing thoughts and feelings...."
    "Speaking to you as a child..."
    "The charming men and women..."
    Punctuation:
    Run on sentences:
    "Take a look at your <u>watch</u> how easily you can change."
    Pause at improper places.
    Incomplete sentences: The sentence is left unfinished
    "I know that you're considering. . . ."

19. **Utilisation:**
    Utilise all that happens or is said by stating what is verifiable.
    Client says: **"I can't change."**
    Response: **"That's right. You can't change yet, because you haven't experienced the trance that will allow you to make the unconscious changes without even having to think about changing."**

Putting it all together:

"Because (Cause and Effect) you can find it so easy to relax, you can now realise.... (Punctuation) Everybody (Universal Quantifier) can, it can be so easy (Unspecified verb). On many levels, all of the time, you are changing many, many things ...should (Modal Operator) you really want to...your new learning's...and you can...won't you? (Tag Question) It's good to change (lost performative) Many people can learn (Lack of referential index)... and as you sit there, listening (Pacing current experience), I know (Mind read) how you can do so much better now (Comparative Deletion). You can listen to me or not at all. You can relax or you may choose to delay your relaxation (Nominalisation) ...until now (Double Bind). Do you realise that this is something you can do easily (Conversational Postulate), the chair is feeling depressed (Syntactic), as your eyes become heavier...have you ever listened to the birds singing in the trees (Presupposition)....the message that they bring from the butterflies who have spoken to the whispering winds (Selectional Restriction) who are telling you (Extended Quote) "here (Phonological) you can hear me speaking to you as a child. (Scope) If you know that moving mountains is not easy for you ...then it can be done (Complex Equivalence), that's right your breathing is accepting this possibility...""(Utilisation)

Create a script using at least 12 of the above patterns. www.peoplebuilding.co.uk and download one of the free Hypnosis scripts. See what Milton Model patterns can be identified in the script.

Hypnotic patterns

Hypnotic patterns were used by Milton Erickson, who was largely responsible for bringing hypnosis into the clinical world. He was a master of indirect suggestion, which means he could induce trance in a client, in a more conversational way, than the direct "GO INTO A TRANCE" and swinging watch techniques that had occurred earlier.

Direct and indirect suggestion

(The difference between Direct and Indirect)

A direct suggestion appeals to the conscious mind which is able to evaluate. E.g. "Listen very carefully."

An Indirect suggestion goes straight to the unconscious mind and is not evaluated as much. E.g. "I wonder if you can *listen very carefully*."

Embedded Commands

These are scattered in conversations/ sentences to bypass the conscious mind.

"I hope you are able to *finish your thoughts on time*."

Truisms about sensations

"Most people are pleased when they discover something they didn't know."

"People often want things."

"I am relieved when I get things done that need doing."

Truisms utilising time

"*Sooner or later* you're going to understand."

"Looking back to the days gone by, you realise that **today** you know so much more than you did **yesterday,** or even just **a few moment ago**."

Not knowing, not doing

"You don't have to learn your homework, you don't even have to do your homework, but if you want to be successful in life then you know what you have to do."

"You don't even have to consciously listen."

"You can daydream and not know you are awake."

Open ended suggestions

"All people have potential they are unaware of, and they don't usually know when they will be going to use it."

"He doesn't yet know the power of what he is learning, but he is still learning. And who am I to say to him "learn this" or "learn that." He'll learn in just the right way, in just the way he wishes."

Covering all possibilities of responses

"Soon you'll discover a way of understanding this. Perhaps you'll learn from me, or maybe someone you know or someone you don't know will inspire you, or you may find the answers within yourself. Just realise the importance of your understanding."

Questions that facilitate new response possibilities

a) To focus attention

"Did you experience trance as similar or different to the waking state?"

b) Facilitating internal change

"Did you notice after you had tidied away the clutter around you how much clearer you were feeling as you enjoyed the space inside?"

Compound suggestions

a) Yes set

"You want to learn NLP; you understand how the techniques

can work for you. We have arranged a payment scheme, are there any other questions before you sign up?"

b) Associations

"With each breath that you take you become more aware of the natural rhythm of your body and the feelings of comfort that develop."

c) Opposites

"The more you listen to me, the less interested you'll be in what others have to say."

d) Negative tag question

"And you can, can you not?"

"You can try, can't you?"

"You can't stop it, can you?"

"Why not let that happen?"

e) Negative until

"You don't have to do Trance Forming Minds Hypnosis training until you've finished your NLP Master Practitioner Training with People Building."

f) Shock, surprise

"Having wind (pause) lets the gas out of these problems. Secretly you know the winds of change are coming."

Implication and Implied Directive (if... then... statements)

a) "If you sit down then you can get ready to change."

b) "Now, if you uncross your legs and place your hands comfortably on your lap, then you will be ready to enter a trance."

Binds and Double Binds

a) Approach – Avoidance: "Would you like to go ahead now or when I call you back later."

b) Conscious – unconscious: "I think that your unconscious mind knows more about that than your conscious mind does, and if you're unconscious mind knows more about it than your conscious mind does, then you probably know more about it than you think you do."

c) "I think that your heart wants to do this as much if not more than your head. Now we all need to quiet our mind sometimes but no-one should stop their heart wouldn't you agree?"

d) Double-dissociation double bind

"You can make a decision to come to People Building NLP Training without being aware of it consciously then you can be surprised in the next few minutes how much you really want to do this."

Varieties of Double Binds

Binds are a free choice of two or more comparable alternatives.
Double Binds are used for offering possibilities that would usually be outside of normal conscious choice and control. Double binds are used to create multilevel communication. The bind may be created using language only or a combination of verbal and non-verbal communication.

Common Components of Double Binds:
1. Using conscious/ unconscious dissociation
2. Creating positive Internal Representations
3. Use of exclusive/ inclusive OR
4. Marking out using voice, gesture or tone.

Rossi's study of Double Binds (From Ernest Rossi's studies of Milton Erickson):
1. Make a statement
2. Make a Meta comment about the statement.

"Would you like to experience trance now or later? Everyone does and as soon as you have you can realise it was exactly what you needed now."

Types of Double Binds
1. Question
"Would you like to listen or watch to learn, or do both?"

2. Time Bind
"....now or after you have rested?"

3. Conscious/ Unconscious Double Bind
a) "If you're unconscious wants you to listen, it will shut off all sounds, otherwise you'll hear me with those sounds."
b) "You need not make an effort to follow my instructions. You're unconscious mind can process the instructions without

any effort from you at all."

c) "If you want to learn hypnosis you'll just know. Otherwise looking at the course content for Trance Forming Minds would be of interest to you."

4. Double-dissociation double bind

a) "You can listen, but you can do so, as if out of your body and far away. Then later, when you return, you'll come back with all of the knowledge that you heard, without even knowing how you got it."

b) "You can make notes on what you hear. Hearing it from a different place where there is only total understanding, and keeping that with you after you have heard it."

5. Reverse set double bind

"Not" + Positive internal representation of desired behaviour.

a) "Don't even think about planning your life as a wealthy NLP Master Practitioner."

b) "Don't do it; sign up for Trance Forming Minds Hypnosis Training, wait until you've finished reading the book!"

6. Non-sequitur double binds

a) "I can do whatever we want, it's your decision."

b) "You can choose to change when I'm ready to give you the instruction to do so. Not changing will only cause unhappiness and both of us want to be happy."

7. Suggestions covering all possibilities

"You may choose to learn or not learn here, now. You might decide that now is the right time to learn or perhaps later, maybe not at all. Either way, even by not learning you will have learned all of the things you choose not to know."

Create a Double Bind for each of the examples above for therapy, business or education.

Transformational Metaphors

Metaphors are stories with hidden meaning that are designed entirely for unconscious understanding. This means that whilst the conscious mind is attempting to untangle the messages, the messages to suggest change are implanted into the unconscious, where all behaviours and habits are stored.

Metaphors work best when they contain lots of sensory-based words, when they use symbols (the unconscious uses and responds to symbols, when we dream for example) and when they are based around a clients interests, such as a particular hobby.

1. **Build Rapport**

2. **Gather information:**
a) What's the problem?
b) What do you want instead?
c) What stops you having it now?
d) What's most important to you?
e) What do you most enjoy?
f) What hobbies/ interests do you have?

3. **Lateral Chunking:**
a) What is this an example of?
b) What are other examples of this?

4. Create a bridge from the Present State to the Desired State in a way that there can be no conscious connection.

5. Deliver the Metaphor.

Write a metaphor for someone who wants to quit smoking and enjoys travelling to exotic places. Include at least 9 of the previous language patterns.

The Dreamweaver Process

The process below is used to help you create a metaphor. During the consultation, gather all of the key components of the problem and list them in column 1. Then for each components think of a symbol that represents that. In column 3, write or draw a symbol that represents the symbol in column 2.

Use the symbols in column 3 to create a metaphor.

Desired deep meaning for metaphor:

All key components and relationships.	What is a symbol for each of the components in column 1?	In the desired context, what is a symbol for each of the components in column 2?
1	**2**	**3**
E.g. Heights	Sky scraper	Hotel
Fear	Face	Smile
Shortness of breath	Mask	Make up
Heart pounding	Heart shape	Colour red
Sweaty hands	Hand print	Finger print

For example:

"A friend of mine visited the most magnificent hotel. It was once where lots of famous people stay, in the centre of town. The security there was amazing, guards on the doors to make *you feel really safe* they even take a copy of your fingerprint when you check in.

The customer service was great too, the girls behind the receptions desk were as pristine as airhostesses in their bright red suits, their glamorous makeup...telling me that I can *relax and have a very enjoyable experience.....*"

> Think of a phobia for which you could use this process to create a metaphor. Then write the metaphor using the symbols you list in column 3.

Nested Loops

Firstly   Then, sometime

later

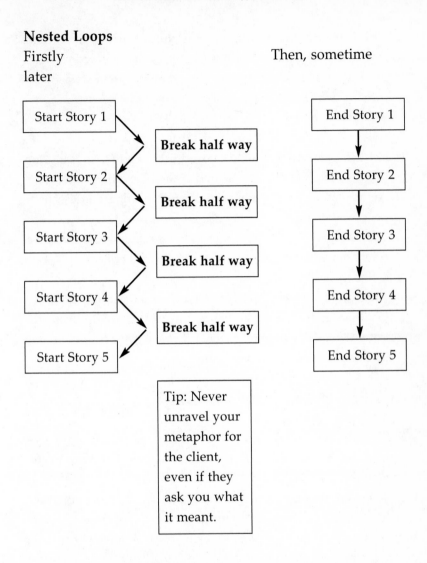

Using the metaphor process above, create 5 stories that can all be linked to each other. Break each story half way through. This could be used during the first session you do with the client.

In the second session, finish each of the stories, starting with the story that you finished last and working backwards. This creates confusion in the client which, as they attempt to figure out why the stories are unfinished will send them into a trance and give the clients mind a strong compulsion to return for the second session as they will have a great urge to seek the completion of the incomplete stories. You may even like to make them wait longer before you deliver the completion of the stories.

A Short Example:

1) Once there was a man who enjoyed listening to the radio. Onc day his daughter retuned the radio and he overheard
2) An advert for a company who offered training that can help people change the way they use their minds
3) You know it's an amazing thing, the mind. Some say that the conscious is like the captain of a ship, and that the unconscious is like the crew of the ship
4) And you know how peaceful it can be, on a ship I mean, looking up into the sky and all of the great space up there
5) I often wonder what life exists in that great space, who might be there bouncing around on the moon.

Break Here, then sometime later continue...

5) So your there bouncing around there...in outer space-whatever next? Perhaps they'll have people building on the moon!
4) And from way up there, you could just see the great oceans of the world... the vastness, with beautiful sailing ships
3) Diligently following very specific instructions from their captains who use
2) NLP to change their thinking, to get new strategies, to advertise themselves to the world in a new way. On the radio perhaps..
1) Where he discovered his station...had re-tuned .. into a clearer frequency.

Representational System Predicates

When you use hypnosis, the experience for your client can be greatly enriched by the use of sensory-based words.

You may identify that your client has a preferred sensory system, by hearing that they tend to use more of a particular range of visual words, for example, or that their eyes move to a certain place regularly to imply that they are spending more time in a sensory system.

If you would like to find out more about eye elicitation patterns or how to test for sensory systems, please visit www.peoplebuilding.co.uk to sign up for NLP Practitioner training where these skills are taught.

Visual	Auditory	Kinaesthetic	Auditory Digital
see	hear	feel	think
revealing	listen	touch	consider
envision	sound(s)	hard	experience
illuminate	make music	turn around	understand
twinkle	harmonise	grasp	learn
clear	tune in/out	get hold of	process
foggy	be all ears	slip through	decide
looking	rings a bell	catch on	motivate
appear	attuned	tap into	consider
view	silence	make contact	change
shown	be heard	throw out	perceive
dawn	resonated	unfeeling	distinct
focused	deaf	concrete	conceive
hazy	mellifluous	scrape	identify
crystal clear	shouts	get a handle on	question
flashed	overtones	solid	be conscious
imagine	unhearing	suffer	logic
picture	outspoken	unbudging	reasonable
sparkling	tells	impression	statistically
snap shot	announce	touch base	analyse
watch	talk	rub	investigate
perspective	speak	smooth	enquiry
frame	resonate	pushy	method
shine	whispering	stumble	procedure
dim	snap	in touch	regard
vivid	hum	relaxed	distinguish
perceive	loud	loose	recognise
light	stated	cool	mindful
ray	whine	tepid	aware
mesmerise	babble	heavy	common sense
image	echo	deep	examine
vision	orchestrate	slip	test
observed	dialogue	depress	study

Further Resources

Remember that you are only restricted by your boundless imagination, and imagination is the key ingredient required for your
scripts. The more inspiring, confusing and engaging your scripts
are, the deeper your client's level of trance will be.

Once you have decided on your idea, you may like to write
your script out in full, or you might like to write notes and trust
your powerful unconscious to do the rest for you when the time
comes.

If you would like to become a professional Hypnotherapist
visit www.peoplebuilding.co.uk then sign- up for the course
below.

Trance Forming Minds 1
- The History of Hypnosis
- The Therapy Movement
- Prime Directives of the Unconscious Mind
- Rapport, Calibration, Pacing, Elicitation
- Pre Hypnosis Consultations
- Suggestibility Tests
- Inductions and Deepeners
- Signs and Symptoms of Trance
- Post Hypnotic Suggestions and Anchors
- Double Binds
- Ericksonian Hypnosis
- Self-Hypnosis
- Resistance and Abreaction

Trance Forming Minds 2
- Brain Structure
- Representational Systems
- Hypnotic Language Patterns

- Linguistic Presuppositions
- Milton Model
- Meta Model
- Levels of Competency
- Smoking Cessation
- Ideomotor Testing
- Regression

Trance Forming Minds 3

- Indirect Techniques
- Stage Hypnosis and Rapid Inductions
- Double Induction
- Hypnotic Metaphors
- Dreamweaver Process
- Common Problems and Hypnotic Resolutions
- Mental Healing
- Ethics and the Law
- Safety in Therapy
- Record Keeping
- Practice Set Up Marketing and Advertising

150 hours on course
3x 10 hour open book tests at home
10 hours reading
Unlimited practice at home

Trance-forming minds is run over three months and is split into 5 days of classroom work each month, with additional tasking which must be conducted in between each course in order to meet the required numbers of hours for certification. There are also several multiple choice tests which you must score over 90% correct answers in each one to pass the course.

The Trance forming Minds course offered by People Building has been assessed and validated at Practitioner Level by The General Hypnotherapy Standards Council (UK). Graduates from